copyright: Copyright b-- ^:

A

This document is geare~ ~~able
information with reg~ ~~p~ and issue covered.
The publication is sold with the idea that the publisher is not
required to render accounting, officially permitted, or
otherwise, qualified services.
If advice is necessary, legal or professional, a practiced
individual in the profession should be ordered.
From a Declaration of Principles which was accepted and
approved equally by a Committee of the American Bar
Association and a Committee of Publishers and Associations.
In no way is it legal to reproduce, duplicate, or transmit any
part of this document in either electronic means or in printed
format.
Recording of this publication is strictly prohibited and any
storage of this document is not allowed unless with written
permission from the publisher.
All rights reserved.
The information provided herein is stated to be truthful and
consistent, in that any liability, in terms of inattention or
otherwise, by any usage or abuse of any policies, processes, or
directions contained within is the solitary and utter
responsibility of the recipient reader.
Under no circumstances will any legal responsibility or blame
be held against the publisher for any reparation, damages, or
monetary loss due to the information herein, either directly or
indirectly.
Respective authors own all copyrights not held by the
publisher.

1

Disclaimer

The Complete Books of Enoch

*The Apocryphal -
The Watchers, Fallen Angels, The
Origin of Evil and The Cosmic
Covenant*

By Christopher David Richardson

Translator: Mark Anthony Rowland

Author: R.H. Charles

Contents

The man, Enoch

Enoch is a biblical figure who appears as Noah's great-grandfather in the Book of Genesis. Enoch lived for 365 years before being taken up to heaven by God, without experiencing death, according to the Bible. Enoch became a popular figure in Jewish and Christian apocryphal, including the Book of Enoch, an ancient text that claims to be written by Enoch himself, as a result of his mysterious departure.

The Book of Enoch is a collection of writings that dates back to the Second Temple period, around 500 BCE to 70 CE. It is considered pseudepigraphical, meaning that it was written under a false name, and is not included in the biblical canon of either the Jewish or Christian faiths. However, the Book of Enoch was highly regarded by some Jewish and Christian groups during this time and has continued to be a source of inspiration and interest for many people throughout history.

Enoch's life and teachings go beyond this simple relationship. He is also considered the father of Methuselah, the longest-lived person in the Bible who lived for 969 years.

The name "Enoch" means "dedicated" or "initiated" in Hebrew, which suggests that he may have been a religious leader or a member of a priestly class. This idea is supported by the Book of Jubilees, which claims that Enoch was the first person to learn how to write and recorded the knowledge he received from the angels.

The Book of Enoch, a religious text attributed to Enoch, was not discovered in its entirety until the 18th century. Prior to that, only fragments of the book were known to exist in Greek, Latin, and Aramaic translations. The Book of Enoch has been cited as an influence on various religious and philosophical movements, including Gnosticism, Kabbalah, and Rosicrucianism.

The Book of Enoch is a unique text that contains a mixture of Jewish and Greek mythological elements, leading some scholars to suggest that it was written in response to the Hellenization of Judea.

Enoch's journey through the heavens and encounters with angels and other supernatural beings are described in the Book of Enoch. It also includes predictions about the end of the world and the arrival of the Messiah.

Enoch appears in a number of other ancient texts, including the Dead Sea Scrolls and Gnostic texts. Enoch is associated with the concept of a "sky god" or a heavenly messenger in some African and Native American cultures. Enoch (also known as Idris in Arabic) is mentioned several times in the Quran as a prophet who lived before Noah. God bestowed great knowledge and wisdom on Enoch, according to Islamic tradition, and he taught his people about the true path of righteousness.

Enoch is also mentioned in the New Testament in the book of Jude, where he is described as a prophet who spoke out against the ungodly behavior of certain individuals.

Enoch remains an enigmatic figure in religious history, whose life and teachings continue to inspire and intrigue people from a variety of cultural and religious backgrounds. His legacy is a reminder of the power of faith and the importance of preserving ancient religious texts for future generations.

Not all of the Ethiopic text was represented. The Book of Enoch is usually divided into five sections , and all sections but one were represented among the pieces. The second section of the Ethiopic text, known as the Similitudes of Enoch, was not there.

This is a very significant gap, as we shall see later, because the Similitudes are a very close relation to much in early Christian thought, and the question which all scholars would like to answer is: 'Were they a Christian composition, or were they an older work which the Christians used?'

It is possible that they were not written until after the Qumran library had been abandoned. It is also possible that the library did not have a copy of every known Enochic work. Another distinct possibility is that the caves had been visited in the past, and books removed. Origen, the great Christian scholar and teacher who lived in Caesarea in the early third century and who died a martyr's death in the persecution of AD 254, found a translation of the Book of Psalms together with other Hebrew and Greek books in a jar near Jericho. Jericho is about ten miles north of Qumran! At the end of the eighth century the Patriarch of Seleucia knew of Old Testament books and others in Hebrew writing which had been found in a rock dwelling near Jericho by an Arab out hunting who followed his dog into a cave. (Seleucia was the port of Antioch; Paul and his companions embarked there on their missionary journey, Acts 13.4.) A ninth-century writer knew of a Jewish sect called 'the Sect of the Cave' because their books were found in a cave. The twentieth-century scholars, then, were not the first to take scrolls from the ancient library of Qumran, and it would be very dangerous to assume that what was not there in the 1950s had never been there in the first place.

Enoch was taken up to heaven twice, once for 60 days and during this time he wrote 366 books. He was first brought up to heaven on the first day of the month of Tsivan. He wrote all the signs of all the creation which the LORD had made, and wrote three hundred and sixty-six books, and gave them to his sons, and abode on the earth for thirty days, and was taken up again to heaven on the sixth day of the month of Zivan. This all is written in the Secrets of Enoch, chapter 68, verse 1-3.

According to Enoch 22:10, the Lord summoned one of his angels, Pravuil, and charged him with writing down all of creation's secrets. Pravuil then recorded all of creation's secrets, and the Lord gave him the book to give to Enoch.

According to Enoch 22:11, the Lord gave Enoch the book and commanded him to read it and teach all of the secrets contained within it to the children of men. Enoch was also told to reveal the secrets of man's creation, the spirit of man, and God's commandments.

Enoch 22:12 states that Enoch began to teach the children of men the secrets of the book, and they began to understand the mysteries of God and the creation of the world. Enoch taught them about the spirit of man, the commandments of God, and the secrets of the creation of the world.

The lost Prophet

Enoch is mentioned as a prophet in the Epistle of Jude in a passage (w. 14-15) where he is said to have prophesied that the Lord would come with his holy myriads to execute judgment on all. Enoch, the seventh generation from Adam, also predicted that the ungodly would be convicted of their ungodly deeds, which they committed in an ungodly manner, and of the harsh words that ungodly sinners have spoken against God.

The biblical figure of Enoch, mentioned in Jude's Epistle, appears only briefly in the Old Testament. Enoch was the son of Jared, the father of Methuselah, and he "walked with God" before God "took him" (Genesis 5.18-24) - which some translations suggest refers to angels instead. Despite this brief mention, an important Enoch cult developed, with the belief that he did not die but was taken up to heaven like Elijah and would be revealed as a messenger of judgment in the last days.

Enoch was a significant figure in Jewish and Christian tradition, and many legends arose about him over time. In Jewish medieval writings, Enoch was regarded as a messianic figure who lived in seclusion until an angel summoned him to teach God's ways. He was exalted to the position of king over the angels, similar to Christ's exaltation in the Christian tradition. Enoch was a wise man to whom the angels revealed the secrets of judgment and natural order in earlier Jewish tradition, and he was associated with astronomy, the calendar, and interceding for the fallen angels. He was also regarded as the heavenly scribe who presided over the books at the final judgment and was given the title "Son of Man," according to another source.

In Christian tradition, Enoch was known as the great scribe and one of the two prophets who oppose the antichrist in the last days, often identified with Elijah. Many Christian writings in various languages show how widely this aspect of the Enoch legend was known, and he even appears occasionally in Christian art, such as a stained glass window in Canterbury Cathedral.

There are several writings associated with Enoch, including 2 Enoch, known as the Secrets of Enoch, a work that has survived only in Old Church Slavonic, and 3 Enoch, a Jewish mystical text. The Book of Enoch, also known as Ethiopic Enoch, is the most well-known, with the entire text surviving only in the Ethiopian language. These books are given modern names by scholars for clarity but do not necessarily reflect their ancient titles.

The main source of information on the book of Enoch is the Ethiopic version discovered by James Bruce, a Scottish explorer who landed in Ethiopia in 1769. In his journals, Bruce describes his discovery of an ancient Christian civilization in Ethiopia, full of churches that every great man felt obliged to build. The churches were round buildings with thatched roofs, hung with pictures but devoid of carvings due to the belief that they breached the second commandment. It was within these churches that Bruce discovered the long-lost book of Enoch the prophet.

It is uncertain how Christianity came to Ethiopia, but it is known that the country had ancient links with Judaism. The royal house of Ethiopia claims descent from King Solomon, and Jewish priests served in the Ethiopian capital city of Aksum. The Queen of Sheba, who had visited King Solomon, had a son by him who became the Ethiopian king Menelik.

The first firm evidence of Christianity in Ethiopia is from the early fourth century when two Christian travelers from Tyre, Frumentius and Aedesius, were taken captive by robbers in an Ethiopian port. They won the people's confidence and preached Christianity, eventually becoming tutors to the young princes and gaining the favor of the royal family. Frumentius was nominated as regent for the young king after the death of his father, and he later returned to Alexandria to recruit more missionaries before being consecrated bishop of Ethiopia.

King Ezana, who reigned in the later part of Frumentius's reign, was also converted to Christianity.

His earlier royal inscriptions had pagan motifs, but his later ones were Christian. In the fifth century, many Monophysite Christians, who believe that the nature of Jesus is wholly divine, fled persecution as heretics after the Council of Chalcedon in 451 and found refuge in Ethiopia. Among them were nine monks with Syrian names who were successful as missionaries in Ethiopia and founded monasteries, translating sacred books. It is possible that this is how the book of Enoch came to Ethiopia. During his travels in Ethiopia, Bruce collected manuscripts and commissioned scribes to copy out others for him, including the book of Enoch.

The discovery of the Dead Sea Scrolls near the Qumran monastery in the northwestern corner of the Dead Sea in September 1952 marked a watershed moment in Enochic studies. The first scrolls were discovered five years prior, when an Arab shepherd boy discovered earthenware jars containing scrolls while throwing stones into cave mouths. The scrolls were later discovered to be fragments of various works, including a complete scroll of the prophet Isaiah and the Genesis Apocryphon, a rewriting of Genesis.

In 1952, a group of Arab herders discussed their new source of income, and an elderly man among them recalled a childhood incident in which he followed a wounded partridge into a cave and discovered an old lamp, several fragments of pottery, and thousands of manuscript fragments buried in the earth. Cave 4 was discovered to be the Qumran settlement's library, or the location where they stored their library when they abandoned their settlement and hid their scrolls. One of the two chambers had been stacked almost full of jars containing manuscripts, including the remains of eleven manuscripts, or part manuscripts, of Enoch.

The fragments did not contain the entire Ethiopic text of the Book of Enoch. The Book of Enoch is traditionally divided into five sections, and all but one were represented among the fragments. The Similitudes of Enoch, the second section of the Ethiopic text, was missing.

This is a significant gap because it is so close to much of early Christian thought. Scholars are divided on whether the Similitudes were written by Christians or were adapted from an older work. It is possible that they were not written until after the Qumran library had been abandoned, that the library did not have a copy of every known Enochic work, or that the caves had been visited in the past, and books removed.

In the past, scrolls from the ancient library of Qumran were taken, and it would be dangerous to assume that what was not there in the 1950s had never been there in the first place.

The Interpretattion and Discussion on Enoch's Book

The Book of Enoch is a strange and fascinating text that describes heavenly visions, journeys through fantastic mountain ranges, and strange versions of Israel's history. While the book is strange and requires explanation, the people who wrote the New Testament used and understood it. The fact that the New Testament writers were perfectly at home in Enoch's world raises concerns about whether we are reading and understanding the New Testament in the way that it was intended.

Unguided Bible study can easily lead to creating God in our own image, and it is important to recognize that the New Testament was not written with modern, everyday English ideas. Reading Enoch in modern English illustrates this problem perfectly and brings us face to face with a whole body of literature for which we have not devised our own ways of understanding.

While some New Testament passages are more frequently used than others, this selection process can distort our understanding of the New Testament. We may be tempted to skip over familiar-sounding sections dealing with social justice and the like in 1 Enoch because we can deal with them. However, if we do so, we will be passing up an excellent opportunity to change our mental picture of the entire thought world of Jesus' time.

Enoch illuminates the New Testament in ways that challenge our familiar picture of Jesus as a simple teacher surrounded by ordinary and largely unlettered folk who withstood the sophisticated religious leaders of their time. 1 Enoch is not a popular work, not the simple religion of Galilean peasants and fishermen. It represents an enormous body of learning, sophisticated in its own way - ancient, intricate, and highly developed.

If the New Testament writers were aware of such teachings, the New Testament may be nothing more than the tip of an iceberg. Because it was already accepted, much of what was important in early Christianity may not be spelled out in the New Testament. As a result, we owe it to ourselves to make an effort to comprehend this strange book and others like it.

The Book of Enoch is attributed to a wise man from the age before Noah's flood, even though he cannot possibly have written it. Such a practice is known as pseudepigraphy, 'writing under a false name.' To the modern mind, it seems like forgery, but if we allow this to color our judgments, many other things will come as an even greater shock. Writing in the name of another, claiming prophetic inspiration in this way, was an accepted thing in New Testament times.

The Book of Enoch is a fascinating text with many similarities and differences to the Old Testament. It appears to represent a type of Judaism that places little emphasis on the temple sacrificial cult and the Law of Moses, but a great emphasis on the day of judgement and Enoch's mediation and revelation. This implies that Enoch was written by a very conservative group with roots dating back to the time the Jewish people returned from Babylon.

Enoch's significance for our understanding of Christianity cannot be overstated. Early Christianity claimed to be the true fulfillment of the Old Testament, and it is likely that ideas about the Messiah were based on earlier kings' hopes and ideals. These earlier ways are echoed in Enoch, and it is not surprising that the book was preserved as a Christian text despite being written long before the time of Jesus.

The fate of Enoch after its writing is also of interest. Some Jewish teachers in the earliest Christian centuries had a negative attitude towards it, while others remembered Enoch as the great scribe in heaven, the archangel Metatron, and a messianic figure. Enoch was a figure who aroused considerable passion, and it is clear that there were those who cherished the traditions associated with him, among them the Christians.

When we compare Enoch to other ancient writings that are not found in the Old Testament, we find that many of them have allusions to the same old traditions that we find in Enoch. This implies that they contain pieces of an ancient jigsaw puzzle of ideas that underpin much of the Old Testament. This hidden pattern underpins the New Testament, which builds on and completes the old traditions. Enoch and other ancient texts, in this way, serve as a vital link between the past and the present, illuminating the foundations of our religious and cultural heritage.

The Book of Enoch, a collection of writings attributed to the biblical figure Enoch, is a source of great interest and debate among scholars. Divided into five sections, only four have been found as fragments among the Dead Sea Scrolls. The missing section, known as the Similitudes or Parables, contains passages that some argue suggest a Christian influence.

The focus on the Son of Man, a title used to describe Jesus in the New Testament, is particularly noteworthy. If the Similitudes are a-Christian, then they may provide insight into early Christian beliefs and the development of the Son of Man concept. However, if the Similitudes are pre-Christian, then they may offer an understanding of what Jesus meant when he referred to himself as the Son of Man.

Scholars have used the absence of the Similitudes among the Dead Sea Scrolls to suggest that they must be post-Christian. However, this argument is flawed as it assumes that the Qumran library had a copy of every known book, which is unlikely. Other Enoch writings have been referenced in other ancient texts, but these cannot be matched to any of the Enoch books found among the Dead Sea Scrolls.

Dating the Enoch books is also a complicated process, as relying solely on the analysis of fragments found at Qumran can be misleading. It is dangerous to assume that these texts were composed at the Qumran monastery and that surviving fragments are from the author's original manuscript. This method of dating would also suggest that the Old Testament was all composed in the second century BC in the Qumran monastery, which is unlikely.

We must have an open mind when considering the dating of the Enoch writings, and not apply one set of rules for the biblical texts and another for non-biblical texts. It is possible that the Enoch writings could be as old as anything in the Old Testament, and we should not dismiss them based on incomplete evidence.

It's worth noting that the Book of Enoch is not accepted as canon by most of the major Christian denominations. However, it was widely read and respected in early Jewish and Christian communities and is quoted in the New Testament book of Jude.

The Book of Watchers

The Book of Enoch, like Genesis and Exodus, is a collection of stories. The Book of the Watchers, the first section, tells the story of the evil angels who came to Earth and corrupted it. The first two chapters of this section, chapters 6-10, tell two stories. One tells the story of Asael, who brought forbidden knowledge to Earth, and the other of Semihazah, who led 200 angels to Earth to marry human wives. These angels' offspring were terrifying demons who infested and corrupted the Earth. For seventy generations, Asael was bound in the desert, while Semihazah's angels were bound in the Earth's valleys.

In chapter 12, Enoch is commissioned to take the message of judgement to the fallen ones. They ask Enoch to intercede for them, but he learns in his heavenly vision that there is to be no mercy for them. The remainder of The Book of Watchers describes Enoch's heavenly journeys, where he sees the secrets of creation. The Book of Enoch is similar to the biblical book of Job in its description of journeys to explore the secrets of the universe.

These two stories are told in the Book of the Watchers without any mention of Enoch. They are simply the setting for what happens next. Then, in chapter 12 , we learn that Enoch is to take to the fallen ones the message of their judgement. Enoch, like the other prophets, is commissioned to announce the imminent judgement of God. Unlike the other prophets, he announces judgement upon the evil angels. The fallen ones ask Enoch to intercede for them, and Enoch is then caught up to heaven in a vision of God. What follows is one of the most remarkable passages in the book (we shall return to it later). In his heavenly vision, Enoch learns that there is to be no mercy for the fallen ones.

The Book of Watchers discusses how Enoch was chosen by God to be a witness to the secrets of heaven. He tells of his vision of the Watchers, angels who have left their proper habitation and taken on human form to marry and have children with human women. God is angry with them for this transgression and decides to punish them by sending them to earth.

Enoch is taken on a tour of the heavens by the angel Uriel. He sees the stars, the sun, and the moon, and is shown the secrets of the calendar and the movements of the celestial bodies. He also sees the spirits of the dead being judged and sent to their final resting places. Enoch is shown the Garden of Righteousness and the Tree of Life.

He is told that those who are righteous will be allowed to partake of the tree and live forever in the presence of God. Enoch is taken to the fifth heaven, where he sees the throne of God and the angels singing praises to him. He is told that the end of the world is near and that God will soon bring judgment upon the earth. Enoch is shown the punishment that will be inflicted upon the Watchers and their offspring, the giants. He is told that they will be bound in chains and thrown into the abyss, never to be released. Enoch is shown the new heaven and earth that will be created after the judgment. He is told that the righteous will live there in peace and happiness forever. Enoch is taken back to earth and told to warn the people of the coming judgment. He preaches to them, but they do not listen and continue in their wicked ways. Enoch is taken up to heaven again and shown the fate of the wicked. He is told that they will be cast into a lake of fire and suffer forever.

We should like to know more about this Asael; he appears in other places in Enoch. In the Similitudes he appears at 55.4, where he is judged by the Elect One as the leader of the evil angels, and yet in 69.2 he is only the twenty-first leader of the bands of angel rebels. In the Book of Dreams, he appears as a fallen star, the first to fall from heaven. The story there suggests that it was Asael who corrupted Adam and Eve in the Garden of Eden, by encouraging them to want the knowledge that had been forbidden to them. The story as we have it now in Genesis 2-3 certainly seems to have a great deal missing from it. We are never told, for example, how the newly created garden came to have an evil serpent in it. Enoch tells us how he got there and who he really was.

The remainder of the Book of Watchers describes Enoch's heavenly journeys when he travels to explore the secrets of the creation. The closest parallel to these journeys is in the biblical book of Job, chapters 38-9. When Job is claiming great wisdom, the Lord speaks to him from a whirlwind and asks if he can know all these secrets of creation. Job admits that he cannot, that such knowledge and the power that it brings belong to God alone. Yet here in Enoch, we find that belief contradicted.

Enoch is given that heavenly knowledge; and the tradition in which he stands, as we shall see, believed that such knowledge conferred angelic status and made one, in effect, like God. Compare this with Genesis 2-3. In the story of the Garden of Eden, the serpent promises Adam and Eve that they would have the knowledge to open their eyes and make them like God. Whoever wrote the Genesis story believed that this knowledge was wrong, and the cause of all subsequent evil. Yet the other, lost tradition says that this knowledge brought one to the presence of God. The wise, like Enoch, walked with God.

The Similitudes

The Similitudes in the Book of Enoch are a collection of visions that offer insight into the nature of the divine and the workings of the universe. These visions are structured around the concept of a great judgement, which will be presided over by a figure known as the Son of Man or the Elect One.

The first vision in the Similitudes describes the throne of God and the four archangels who stand before it. The second vision reveals the nature of the elect and their role in the divine plan. The third vision describes the fall of the angels and their punishment.

The concept of divine justice is one of the Similitudes' most important themes. The great judgement is depicted as a time when the powerful and wealthy will be held accountable for their actions, and the oppressed and downtrodden will be vindicated. This theme is especially pertinent to the social and political context in which the Book of Enoch was written, as the Jewish people faced oppression and persecution at the hands of the Seleucid Empire.

Another key theme in the Similitudes is the nature of the divine. The figure of the Son of Man is portrayed as a divine being who is intimately connected to the Father, and who serves as a bridge between the divine and the human. This figure is also associated with the messianic tradition in Judaism and has been interpreted by some as a precursor to the figure of Jesus in Christian theology.

The Similitudes' use of apocalyptic imagery and symbolism is also noteworthy. Strange and fantastical creatures, cosmic battles, and supernatural phenomena abound in the visions, heightening the sense of drama and urgency surrounding the impending judgement. The Book of Enoch's Similitudes provide a rich and complex vision of the divine and the workings of the universe. They shed light on the nature of justice, the role of the elect, and the relationship of the divine and the human.

Their use of apocalyptic imagery and symbolism also makes them a fascinating example of the apocalyptic genre in ancient Jewish literature.

The parables in the book are presented as visions that Enoch receives from God and are meant to convey moral and spiritual teachings. These parables include descriptions of the end of the world, the judgment of the wicked, and the elect who will be saved. The book also includes a section called the "Astronomical Book," which describes the movement of the stars and the structure of the universe. The Book of Enoch's Parables have had a significant influence on Jewish and Christian apocryphal literature and have been quoted by early Christian writers such as Tertullian and Justin Martyr. The text was also popular among early Christians and was widely read in the early church. However, it was later rejected by mainstream Christianity and is not considered part of the canon of scripture by most Christian denominations. The text is also important to certain sects of Christianity such as Ethiopian Orthodox Church, which consider it as a canonical text, and also some modern scholars has been studied it as a source of historical and religious information.

The Astronomy Book

The third section of the Book of Enoch, chapters 72-82, is known as The Astronomy Book. The fragments of this section found at Qumran show that it was once far longer than the version we now have. The angel Uriel reveals to Enoch all the laws which govern the movements of the heavenly bodies.

The ancient world did not separate science and religion, and wise men like Enoch learned in all knowledge of their day. This included medicine, mathematics, metallurgy, engineering, magic, astrology, and reading omens. For them, all knowledge was knowledge of God's creation, and it was important to know and observe God's laws. In this part of the book, Enoch is told about the true calculation of the calendar, which had to be based on the sun. The restored community in Jerusalem adopted a lunar calendar, which offended the conservative elements of the population. The calculations to establish the calendar were complex and apparently a secret.

Enoch's Astronomy Book warns against leaving out the extra day every quarter that was necessary to keep the calendar even approximately correct. Sinners who alter the calendar upset the whole order of creation, and this is seen as another manifestation of angelic revolt. Nobody can say for certain where this system of reckoning originated, but it may well be peculiar to Israel. Studying the stars was also important for predicting future events, as the stars represented kings, and each king had his own guardian angel who was also a star. The wise men knew the fates of kings and could predict their future in the stars. The Astronomy Book reveals the ancient belief that stars and their movements were part of the great cosmic covenant, bound by the fixed laws of God, except for the evil rebels.

The most famous of disputes in the Astronomical book is the moon-based calendar, and some of the additional parts of the Astronomy Book found at Qumran do in fact deal with the relationship between solar and lunar calendars.

The account as we have it in the Ethiopic version has no polemic about this new calendar; perhaps it comes from a time before this dispute arose, or after it had been resolved. Enoch's Astronomy Book simply warns against leaving out the extra day every quarter which was necessary to keep the calendar even approximately correct.

Each season of the year had a patron angel who had his special day, and within each season there were three other angels, each ruling a month of thirty days. Thus each quarter was 3x304-1, i.e. 91 days, giving a year of 364 days. This was exactly fifty-two weeks, to fit with the seven-day week pattern of the Jewish calendar. Sinners, warns the angel, will alter the calendar so that things will no longer happen at the proper time, the stars will not rise and set when they should, and the whole order of creation will be upset.

This is seen as a revolt of the stars against their proper order, i.e. as another manifestation of angelic revolt: And in the days of the sinners the years shall be shortened, And their seed shall be tardy on their lands and fields, And all things on the earth shall alter, And shall not appear in their time: And the rain shall be kept back And the heaven shall withhold it [...] And the moon shall alter her order, And not appear at her time [...] And many chiefs of the stars shall transgress the order (prescribed). And these shall alter their orbits and tasks, And not appear at the seasons prescribed to them. (I Enoch 80.2, 4, 6).

25

Book of Dreams

The Book of Dreams, which comprises chapters 83-90 of Enoch, tells the story of two dream visions that Enoch recounts to his son Methuselah. The first dream depicts the destruction of the earth, while the second, much longer, depicts Israel's history. The dream becomes more detailed as it approaches the time of the Maccabean revolt in 167 BC, implying that those events were part of God's plan to bring about the Messiah's kingdom and great judgement.

Enoch's history, unlike Daniel's, concludes with great judgement, as the book tells the story of Israel as an animal fable, with Adam as a white bull, Jacob's sons as sheep, and Israel's enemies as eagles, vultures, ravens, and other birds. Angels are depicted as "men" or "men in white," and the book claims that Noah, Moses, and Elijah were born as animals but rose to become angels. In the New Testament and early Christian writings, "men in white" are used to represent those who belong to heaven rather than earth. The Essenes, who dressed in white, saw themselves as living the angelic life. According to Enoch, the righteous will wear garments of glory and garments of life.

The Book of Dreams divides Israel's history into periods, each under the charge of a shepherd, who is an angel figure. The concept of angels, especially guardian angels, is important in early Christian symbolism and practices, and is illustrated in the custom of wearing white christening robes for babies.

The history of Israel in the Book of Dreams is divided into periods, as in Daniel, and each is in the charge of a shepherd, an angel figure. Angels, especially guardian angels, are often called shepherds in this tradition. As early as Ezekiel 34 the guardians of Israel are described as shepherds, and the pastoral imagery of Psalm 23 may mean more than we think. King David had been a shepherd, it is true, and he might naturally have chosen to describe the Lord in this way, but this must not make us overlook the other possibility.

The Lord was regarded as the guardian angel of his people. This is what is meant by the name 'the Holy One of Israel'. As a guardian angel, he would also have been called their shepherd. There is an early Christian book called 'The Shepherd of Hennas' which was written in Rome in the middle of the second century and included in some early versions of the New Testament. It describes the visions given to Hennas by a shepherd angel who is described exactly as a shepherd, wearing a white goatskin, and carrying a shepherd's bag and staff.

The Book of Epistles

The Epistle of Enoch also reveals that the theology of the Enoch writings evolved over time. For example, in the Book of the Watchers, the reward for righteousness was a prosperous old age, while in the Epistle, the righteous were promised to live among the hosts of heaven, similar to the wise in Daniel 12.3 who would shine like the stars. This belief in life after death caused great friction, as the enemies of the Enochic circle did not believe in the last judgement or life after death, but rather took their present prosperity as a sign of God's favor.

Additionally, the Enoch group was not opposed to temple worship per se, but only to the actual temple and its practices, as seen in the later Epistle's emphasis on the renewal of the temple as a sign of the last days. The cleansing of the temple in the Gospels was also seen as a declaration of judgement.

The Apocalypse of Weeks, which is embedded within the Epistle, is another account of Israel's history divided into weeks, with a pattern of sevens or seventies. This reflects the ancient belief that history does not end at the present, but rather at the final judgment, with numerical patterns indicating where they were in the overall scheme. The righteous would triumph in weeks eight, nine, and ten of the Apocalypse of Weeks, with the temple rebuilt and the angels judged.

These Enochic writings provide important insight into Christian ways of thinking, as many of their ideas have passed into Christian doctrine. The familiarity of their language and patterns in the New Testament and regular services can obscure the original meaning and impact of these ancient texts.

In ancient times, there were those who worked wickedness and gloried in deceit, who perverted the language of righteousness and violated the everlasting law. They were warned that they would perish and have no good life. Those who worshiped idols and unclean spirits were also warned that they would receive no support and would ultimately perish.

On the other hand, those who embraced wisdom and walked in the path of righteousness were blessed. Woe was also pronounced on those who spread evil to their neighbors, engaged in deceitful and false deeds, and built their houses through the labor of others. Additionally, those who denied the measure and inheritance of their ancestors and whose souls obeyed idols were warned they would have no rest. Ultimately, it was warned that those who engaged in wickedness and oppression would be punished by the sword and their sins would be remembered by the saints and the righteous. The passage seems to be warning about the consequences of moral decay and the importance of living a virtuous life.

Enoch's encounter and The Vision of God

Enoch ascends to heaven in the Book of the Watchers, sees God's great throne, and then travels through the heavens, observing their secrets. The descriptions in these chapters have resulted in a radical rethinking of the religious scene in the pre-Christian centuries. There is no doubt that the chapters describe a mystical ascent; they are related to later mystical texts that describe God's great chariot throne. Nobody had realized how old these mystical practices were.

According to 1st Enoch 14, Enoch is carried up to heaven by clouds, mists, and winds. He sees a crystal wall surrounded by fire, followed by a crystal house with a ceiling of stars and lightning and fiery cherubim. There was a second house of fire within this one, with a crystal throne, shining wheels, and more cherubim. Streams of fire flowed from beneath the throne, and the Great Glory sat atop it in gleaming white robes. There were ten thousand angels in front of him. Enoch was told to enter by one of the holy ones. The Great Glory told him to take a message of judgement to the Watchers who had left heaven to take human wives, and had thus lost their angelic status and their eternal life.

Enoch is then taken on a heavenly journey to see the treasuries of the stars, the source of the lightning, the mouths of the rivers, and deep. He sees the foundations of the earth and the winds which blow and cause the stars to move. He sees six fabulous mountains of jewels, surrounding the mountain of the throne of God, which has a sapphire summit. He sees the fiery abyss, and the burning mountains which are evil angels, and he is told the names and dudes of the seven archangels. On a second journey, Enoch sees the chaos of darkness and the prison of the angels; he sees the three smooth places where the souls of men assemble for judgement, divided according to whether or not they have received their just deserts on earth.

He sees the Tree of Life waiting to be returned to the Holy Place in Jerusalem, and he sees mountains and valleys, plantations of fragrant trees, and the doors through which the winds blow various weathers.

The experience of ascent is a recurring phenomenon in many cultures, with the ascent and revelation pattern being the record of a genuine experience for most writers. Experiences similar to the ascent of Enoch have been described by people under the influence of certain drugs, and we know that the experiences can be induced in several ways. What is important is not the raw experience itself, but the way in which it has been interpreted. Visions were fundamental in early Christianity and several of the ideas generated by these visions appear in the New Testament. The Old Testament was compiled, edited, and censored, with a line drawn at some point to set apart the 'holy' texts. The Book of Jubilees shows an earlier stage of this process of adapting Scripture. The vision of God was a very ancient practice, yet some Jews saw the type of Jewish religion in which Christianity had its roots as heretical even before the time of Jesus. One of the crucial issues was the vision of God, whether it was possible and what it meant.

To explore the relationship between creation, revelation, and judgment, we must investigate the historical origins of ascent visions in Israel's history. Unlike what was previously believed, the kings of Jerusalem, not the prophets, were the ones who started these visions. Clues found in passages such as Psalm 89.19, 1 Kings 3, and Psalm 2 suggest that the anointed kings of Jerusalem were given wisdom and could ascend to the presence of God, as well as having angelic status. The Messiah in the New Testament, then, could have referred to the anointed one who enjoyed the presence of God and had the status of an angel. These visions were closely tied to the temple, which was believed to be the place of the heavenly throne and the site of the heavenly Garden of Eden. Ezekiel, Isaiah, and John all had temple visions, which included descriptions of trees and cherubim, the throne of God, the seven-branched candlestick, and the river of the water of life.

Finally, the vision of judgment described in Daniel 7 also takes place in the temple, featuring a figure like a son of man ascending to the throne to be given dominion and power for the great judgment. The early Church used this imagery to depict Jesus as the Son of Man and Judge.

The Fourth Gospel portrays Jesus as a royal figure, the Son of God and the King of Israel. He is the earthly representative of God, and his will is the will of God. Jesus is honored with his name and is the earthly manifestation of the glory of God. Those who see Jesus are transformed by the experience and become angelic, living the life of heaven, and passing through death. The Fourth Gospel calls this eternal life, and only those sent by God have seen him. Jesus has the role of the Son of Man, the Judge. The recurring theme of the 'lifting up' of the Son of Man is a clear point of contact with the royal mythology of the angel world. Jesus speaks of those who will have the kingdom of heaven, those who will be sons of God, and those who will see God in the Beatitudes. While Paul also knew this experience of ascent to heaven, his great chapter on love is a criticism of those who placed too much emphasis on it. The Fourth Gospel was written within an Enochic frame of reference, and its points cannot be appreciated if divorced from it. The Jewish background of the writers emphasized the Law and warned against the quest for heavenly knowledge, and the ascent was not possible.

The book of Enoch describes Enoch's vision of the coming of the Messiah and the salvation he will bring to the righteous. Enoch is told that the Messiah will judge the living and the dead. Enoch sees the judgment of the souls of the dead, with the righteous being rewarded with eternal life and the sinners being punished for their crimes. Enoch witnesses the coming of the Lord, who will judge the living and the dead, and sees the end of days when the earth will be purified of all wickedness. The Lord's holy ones will be gathered together and the wicked will be consumed by fire. Enoch sees the Lord's holy ones entering into eternal life, while the wicked are cast into eternal darkness. Enoch also sees the new heaven and the new earth, where the Lord's holy ones will dwell forever in peace and happiness. In his final words, Enoch encourages the reader to walk in the ways of righteousness and to stay away from the ways of wickedness.

When we consider that the oldest section of Enoch contains no criticism of the temple, whereas the later Epistle views temple renewal as a sign of the end times, we can conclude that the Enoch group was not opposed to temple worship in general, but only to the actual temple and its practices (i.e. to the second temple and what it represented). Although early Christians saw another meaning in the saying, Jesus claimed that he would destroy the temple and rebuild it in three days (John 2.19), a prediction of the coming of the judgement in the apocalyptic code. The cleansing of the temple, which all four Gospels record as such an important event in Jesus' ministry, must also have been seen in this light. It was a declaration of judgement; the Lord had come to his temple.

Embedded within the Epistle is another account of Israel's history, divided into weeks and known as the Apocalypse of Weeks as a result. In non-biblical books, there are numerous examples of histories written in a highly artificial form, with everything placed in a pattern of sevens or seventies. This should serve as a warning that their approach to history writing was very different from ours.

For them, history did not end in the present, but at the final judgement, and the strange numerical patterns allowed them to see where their times fit into the grand scheme. They would then know how long it would be before the Lord brought severe punishment on their adversaries. In the Apocalypse of Weeks, there is a great revelation of wisdom in week seven, presumably the author's own time, after which the righteous would triumph, the temple would be rebuilt, and the angels would be judged in weeks eight, nine, and ten. The three heroes are described as 'men' in this history, and those who fell into evil ways are described as blind. In both the Enochic accounts of Israel's history the second temple, built after the return from Babylon, is described as impure, and its devotees as an apostate.

The Cosmic Covenant

The great oath mentioned in the Similitudes of Enoch refers to a cosmic covenant that binds the forces of the creation, securing their order and ensuring their proper functioning. This covenant is entrusted to the archangel Michael and encompasses all aspects of the creation, from the movements of heavenly bodies to the regulation of natural forces like water, wind, and rain. The idea of a cosmic covenant provides a new way of looking at the creation and has relevance for contemporary environmental concerns. Although this aspect of Enochic theology was lost to early Christians, it sheds light on several parts of the New Testament that are no longer understood in their original way. Overall, the great oath represents a primitive yet profound concept that illuminates the significance of order and balance in the natural world.

The text here seems to be in the form of a poem or hymn, with a refrain at the end of each section: And they are strong through his oath: And the heaven was suspended before the world was created, And forever. And through it, the earth was founded upon the water, And from the secret recesses of the mountains come beautiful waters, From the creation of the world and unto eternity.

And through that oath, the sea was created, And as its foundation, He set for it the sand against the time of (its) anger, And it dare not pass beyond it from the creation of the world unto eternity. And through that oath are the depths made fast, And abide and stir not from their place from eternity to eternity. And through that oath, the sun and moon complete their course And deviate not from their ordinance from eternity to eternity. And through that oath, the stars complete their course, And He calls them by their names, And they answer Him from eternity to eternity. And this oath is mighty over them, And through it [they are preserved and] their paths are preserved, And their course is not destroyed, (i Enoch 69.16-21, 25).

The Benedicite, the Song of the Three Children in the Apocrypha, has a very similar theme: all creation praises and acknowledges its Creator. It looks as though there was once far more of the hymn in Enoch than presented survives in the third Similitude; it breaks off rather suddenly. The idea of creating by binding the forces of creation is very ancient, more ancient than the account of the creation we read in Genesis. It is clearly linked to the world of magic, and one which was widely known among ancient peoples. They believed in a cosmic or eternal covenant that kept all things in harmony, in accordance with the divine plan. To break this covenant was to release forces that could destroy the creation. It is interesting that the Hebrew word for covenant, Ifrithy is thought to be related to the word for binding. Some say that this was the binding agreement between two parties, in the manner of the covenant at Sinai. But there could be this other meaning; the binding of the destructive forces. The word for covenant in Hebrew is also very similar to the word 'create'. Covenant bind create makes an interesting sequence in the light of the Enochic picture of creation. Whether or not they are linked we shall probably never know. Closely linked to this oath is the 'name' or the 'secret name', which was the means of enforcing and maintaining the covenant/oath. The name had been named before the creation, presumably to make the creation possible.

The binding of evil has a place in the New Testament. Casting out demons requires that the strong one be bound first (Matt. 12.29). Peter, having recognized Jesus as the Messiah, is given the power to bind and to loose both in heaven and on earth (Matt. 16.13-19). There are several similarities between this story of Peter's commission and Enoch's. (Both happen in the same place, for example.) The most likely explanation of Peter's commission is that he was given power over the evil ones (cf. Luke 10.17, where demons are subjected in Jesus' name, and note the role of the name in the task of binding). The power given to Peter (symbolized by the keys of the kingdom of heaven which now form the papal coat of arms) was later interpreted as the power to bind and loose sins, the power to absolve.

The roots of the idea, however, lie not in forgiving the sin committed by human beings, but in protecting them from evil done to them. The binding was the restraining of evil forces.

This binding of evil spirits to restore the creation is barely distinguishable from the practice of magic, by which is meant not the music-hall tricks of a modern magician, but the more serious practices of dealing with illness and possession. Witch doctors, or perhaps faith healers, are the nearest equivalent we have today. In the ancient world there were many magicians who exorcized as Jesus did, and it is not surprising that non-Christian writers often described Jesus as a magician. The early Church was at pains to separate itself from these people, but the lines were not always distinctly drawn. In addition, the New Testament was written at a time when it was important that the distinction be maintained, and it is quite likely that any ambiguous evidence has been excluded from the accounts. Even so, we have a picture of the early problems. Simon Magus (i.e. Simon the Magician) in Samaria tried to buy the Christian secret (Acts 8.14-24).

The most important passage dealing with creation is Romans 8.14-23. Paul says that we are sons of God (a name pointing us to the angels) because we have received the spirit of sonship. In the account of the fallen angels in Genesis 6 (which is very confusing) the result of the sin is that the spirit of the Lord 'shall not abide in man forever'. Paul reverses this and links the giving of the Spirit with acquiring the status of sonship. Creation waits for the revealing of the sons of God, so that it may be released from bondage to decay. The subjection of creation was the will of God, says Paul, and it is also one of the inexplicable aspects of the apocalyptics worldview that God permits suffering. (The alternative would be to say he was powerless to prevent it, given that suffering exists, and this they would not say.)

In the Book of Dreams, evil shepherds were permitted to harm God's people up to a point, and in the Book of the Watchers, evil demons were permitted to infest the earth until the time came for their judgement.

The new sons of God would be the means by which the former, fallen sons' work would be undone. The process of reversal can be seen in early Christian thought. The Spirit returns and makes new sons of God. They regain the immortality and access to heaven that the first sons of God forfeited by their disobedience, and the creation is restored to its true state of joy. According to Enoch, it is the name and the power of the Son of Man which makes this judgement effective.

This is exactly how Enoch sees a world where the cosmic covenant is broken. Rebel angels, figures of great power, brought knowledge to earth which corrupted and destroyed the creation. The rebel angels had knowledge of technology, medicine and the arts of communication. They were incarnate in political leaders, and those who came under their influence became blind. In his vision Enoch saw the Son of Man restoring the great bonds of creation, healing the rift between earth and heaven, and thus restoring the earth. In less mythological language, we might say bringing beliefs and values into a scientific society which are neither derived from it nor limited by it.

The miracle of healing in John 9 shows how deeply this worldview permeates the Gospels. A man had been born blind, not because of any sin, but so that the power of God could be shown. Jesus healed him. When his eyes were opened, people were wary of him because Jesus did not have the authentication of the establishment. Jesus asked the blind man if he believed in the Son of Man. Why should Jesus have asked about the Son of Man when there had been a healing of blindness? If we read the Fourth Gospel in the light of 1 Enoch and its theology, we realize that the ending of blindness was a sign that the power of evil was being broken and the cosmic covenant was being restored. This was the role of the Son of Man.

The Origin of Evil

Our ideas about the nature and cause of evil are a very important part of our ideas about religion as a whole. We cannot imagine a popular evangelist preaching without once mentioning sin, nor the Roman Catholic Church without the practice of confession. We cannot imagine Christianity without its enormous emphasis upon sin, by which we mean the sin of individual acts and attitudes, doing what we ought not to do, and not doing what we ought to do. The effect of all this emphasis upon the person has been the neglect of the wider, we might say the cosmic, side of our faith.

Christians were hard-pressed to find anything really well-rooted to say about the ecological crisis when this first became a topic of concern in the 1960s. We had no basis upon which to make suggestions, because, for better or worse, our attitudes to the creation had been colored, whether or not we took it literally, by the story in Genesis. Man had been given the earth to master and subdue; it was his to do with as he saw fit.

He had been told to multiply and had been happy to set about this. The crisis, which came from man's domination of the earth and his zealous fulfilment of the command to breed, came as a shock. Mother earth had had enough. The New Testament gives us virtually nothing to work on for a characteristically Christian contribution to the debate. The teaching attributed to Jesus deals with birds and lilies (Matt. 6.25-9) and the value of sparrows (Matt. 10.29-31); Paul speaks about creation in language we do not understand, because we have no certain frame of reference for his ideas (Rom. 8.18-25; Col. 1.15-20). 1 Enoch makes a significant contribution.

It offers another account of the origin of evil, another myth to serve as the pattern for our thinking, and another picture of mankind's role in the created order. Since 1 Enoch was known and used by the first Christians, the ideas in it may well bridge the all-too-obvious gap in the New Testament on this important matter.

In addition, the worldview of 1 Enoch does fit very well as a background to Paul's argument in Romans 8, and this must strengthen the case for its being a long-lost piece of New Testament background material

The question of the origin of evil is a complex and difficult one and has been the subject of much theological debate throughout history. The idea that evil is the result of human sin is only part of the story and does not account for the existence of cosmic evil, which is not the result of human actions.

The question of whether God created evil or not is a contentious one. Some theologians argue that God created everything, including evil, as part of a larger plan or as a necessary aspect of free will. Others argue that evil is a result of the fall of humanity and that God did not create it but allowed it to exist as a consequence of human sin.

The idea that evil in creation was the work of a hostile God was rejected by mainstream Christianity, but the problem of cosmic evil remains. Theologians have tried to address this issue, but no single answer has been accepted as definitive.

The story of Adam and Eve in Genesis is often used to explain the origin of evil, but this is not the only perspective in the Bible. The book of Revelation, for example, provides a different account of the end of evil. Furthermore, the people of Jesus' time did not necessarily interpret the Adam and Eve story as Christians do today. While their story may provide a useful framework for understanding human sin, it does not fully account for the existence of cosmic evil.

The concept of cosmic evil was closely associated with the idea of evil angels and Satan's forces, who were thought to be actively working to corrupt and destroy the creation during Jesus' time. People required defense against this onslaught as well as assistance in overcoming its effects. This worldview contrasts sharply with the more secular and rationalistic approach that characterizes modern society, where evil forces are frequently dismissed as superstition or turned into a form of entertainment.

The book of Revelation, which describes the conflict of the faithful with Satan and other evil powers, reflects this earlier view of the world. It describes the ultimate defeat of Satan and the triumph of the forces of good, leading to a new heaven and a new earth. This is similar to the pattern we find in other ancient texts, such as the Book of Enoch, where the righteous are rescued from the power of the fallen angels and the earth enjoys prosperity and peace.

It is important to recognize that the concept of sin and evil is not static and has evolved over time. Our understanding of these concepts is shaped by our cultural and historical context, as well as by our personal experiences and beliefs. It is also important to recognize that different cultures and religious traditions have different ways of understanding and dealing with sin and evil, and that each approach has its own strengths and weaknesses. Ultimately, what is important is to find a way to live a meaningful and ethical life in the face of the challenges of evil and suffering that we all encounter.

It is true that the New Testament presents a multifaceted view of evil, including the idea of a cosmic conflict between good and evil powers. Jesus is depicted as engaging in this conflict and healing people who were possessed by demons or suffering from illness, which was often seen as a result of demonic influence. The healing ministry was a vital part of Jesus' work, and the command to cast out demons was given to his disciples as well.

It is also true that the Adam and Eve story is not mentioned in the Old Testament outside of the book of Genesis. This has led some scholars to question whether the story was added to the Old Testament at a later stage and whether it was intended to serve as an explanation for sin and evil. The Adam and Eve story does describe human disobedience as the cause of evil, but the idea of inheriting Adam's sin is not a biblical one.

In any case, the important thing to remember is that the New Testament presents a nuanced view of evil, which includes the idea of a cosmic conflict between good and evil powers, the healing ministry of Jesus, and the command to cast out demons.

40

These aspects of the New Testament are often overlooked or neglected, but they are an important part of the Christian tradition and can offer valuable insights into the nature of sin and evil.

Enoch's explanation for the origin of evil is complex, with multiple strands intertwined. One thread concerns the fall of the angels, who became corrupted as a result of pride and self-will. Another thread concerns the heavenly knowledge passed down to humanity by Asael, a powerful angel who knew the secrets of creation. This knowledge bestowed upon humans godlike powers, which they used to corrupt the earth by extracting metals from rock and fabricating weapons of war and seductive ornaments.

Enoch also describes how two hundred angels, led by Semihazah, looked down from heaven and lusted after the beautiful daughters of men. They came to earth to rape them and father half-breed children who were monsters and demons. This resulted in the abuse of women and the corruption of creation.

In later 'wisdom' writings, knowledge/wisdom was regarded as the feminine or creative aspect of God. Enoch's account reflects this idea, as the abuse of wisdom is paralleled by the abuse of women and the corruption of creation. The insight is profound, despite its bizarre expression. It reveals that the urge to power can manifest itself in the abuse of the feminine, creative aspect of God, and this can have devastating consequences on the world we live in.

Even within the Enochic writings, the myth of the fallen angels and their teachings became an important framework for interpreting contemporary situations and issues. The corrupt priesthood of the second century BC, for example, was condemned by comparing them to angels who lusted and took earthly wives. This was a natural application of the angel myth because priests were thought to perform heavenly rituals in the temple, which was viewed as a representation of heaven on earth. The pride and abuse of power that led to the fall of the angels were also seen as relevant to issues of power and authority in human society.

These myths were not simply ancient tales, but a living tradition of theology that provided a way of understanding the world and its problems.

The conflict with evil was not simply exorcism, but also healing. We tend to think of them separately, but in New Testament times they were aspects of one healing process. There was, for example, a relationship between the words blind, lame, deaf, and dumb and the names of the various categories of evil angels. We do not know exactly how this relationship worked, but in each case, the Hebrew name for the angel is similar to that for the affliction. Thus 'Watcher' in Hebrew is the name for an evil angel, but it is also very like the word for the blind. We know from Enoch's Book of Dreams that people under the power of the Watchers became blind. Jesus' healing of blindness was a sign that the power was broken. Other angel names corresponded to lame, deaf, and dumb. When we consider what a large number of Jesus' healing miracles were concerned with just these afflictions, we realize that there was more to the conflict with evil than straightforward exorcism. This evil showed itself in physical disabilities.

The New Testament is so familiar to us that we can easily miss this all-pervasive world of angels. Look at the angel elements in Matthew's Gospel, for example.

We have wise men and a star, Joseph warned by angels in a dream, the conflict with Satan in the temptation story, healing and exorcizing throughout the Gospel, the command to love enemies and so be sons of the Father (i.e. like angels), Capernaum brought to Hades on the day of judgement (like the fallen cities whose guardian angels had been cast out), the secrets of the Kingdom of Heaven, the angel reapers of the last judgement, the righteous shining like the sun (i.e. exalted to heaven and transformed), blind guides, the power to bind and loose in heaven and on earth, little ones with guardian angels in heaven, cleansing the temple (the earthly counterpart of heaven and the scene of the Judgement), the question about divorce with the answer that angels do not marry, the apocalyptic predictions of the fate of Jerusalem and the coming of the Son of Man, and the angel at the tomb on Easter morning.

Everywhere there are angels, or ideas which we now know are associated with them. We cannot possibly read this Gospel without taking the angelic setting into account.

The most vivid point of contact with the Enochic tradition is the parable in Matthew 25, where the sheep and the goats gather before the great throne, awaiting a sentence. The evil ones go to the fire which has been prepared for the devil and his angels (Matt. 25.41). In 1 Enoch 90.20-27 we also read of a judgement before the great throne. Those awaiting judgement are described as sheep (all the human beings in this section are depicted as animals), and they are condemned to the fiery abyss, along with the seventy wicked shepherd angels. In other places our emphasis upon a great sacrifice for our personal sins has led us to overlook the equally important picture of a sacrifice to protect us from threatening evil. A sacrifice for personal sins belongs to the world of the Law and personal responsibility for our actions, whereas a sacrifice to afford protection belongs to a world of threatening evil.

The earliest Christians were all too well aware of the evil all around them. In 1 Corinthians 5.7, we find an early Christian hymn that describes Christ as the Passover lamb which has been sacrificed. The Fourth Gospel implies the same thing; Jesus was killed at the time when the Passover lambs were killed (John 19.14,31).

Now the Passover sacrifice symbolized many things: release from slavery, or the beginning of a new life as the people of God; but as originally described in Exodus 12, the blood of the Passover lamb protected people from the angel of death. The first Christians saw the death of Jesus as a protection against the ever-threatening powers of evil, whose ultimate triumph was corruption and death.

Thus, Colossians 2.15 says that on the cross, Christ overcame the universe's threatening powers; he overcame death. The entire chapter of Colossians is devoted to the cult of the angels and the threat it posed to Christianity.

The nearly incomprehensible argument in Hebrews 1 is also based on beliefs about Christ being greater than the angels, though we no longer know what these beliefs and arguments were. According to 1 Peter 3.22 and Philippians 2.5-11, the powers of heaven have been subjected to Jesus. According to 1 John 3.8, the Son of God came to destroy the devil's work.

Unfortunately, the Old Testament does not answer all the questions we should like to put to it, and we have to do the best we can with what we have. The classic definition of wisdom is that of the opening verses of the book of Proverbs, but even this does not tell us what the learning and skills actually comprised. Job 28 takes us a little further. In describing the things which are not true wisdom (which for the poet is the fear of the Lord), we have some clues as to what others believed wisdom to be. It was mining and engineering skills, perhaps commerce too. The wisdom of the king of Tyre was certainly shown as commercial skill, a skill which he abused. The wisdom of the evil angels in Enoch's account was the knowledge of medicine, the production of metals used to make weapons, knowledge of writing, knowledge of magic, and the control of men's minds and actions.

The fallen angels could manifest themselves in their earthly agents, the blind, or in political leaders as 'the angels of the nations'. They possessed authority because they were wise. The wise men, who were also thought to have access to heavenly knowledge, were kings' advisers. They interpreted men's dreams and predicted their futures for them.

In other words, they were both shapers of ideas and holders of knowledge. According to Enoch's theology, all of this was corrupted when evil angels chose to corrupt the created order and set themselves up as gods. It's no surprise that the most common comment on wisdom in the Old Testament is that fear of the Lord is the beginning of wisdom. The Messiah was expected to fight and protect his people from these looming evils. However, if Christians are also called to be God's sons, the logic of Paul's argument in Romans 8 becomes clear. The entire corrupt and suffering creation awaited the new sons of God to free it from the bonds of evil, not just physical evil, but every abuse of its secrets.

44

This cosmic aspect of the battle entails looking at modern manifestations of wisdom and knowledge (which, surprisingly, are similar to Enoch's) and guarding against corruption by wise men who believe they are gods. We must investigate commercial and industrial practises, medicine, the manufacture of weapons, the various aspects of communication (writing), the formation of opinions (dream interpretation), and the abuse of women (taking the daughters of men). Above all, we must consider political leaders as well as the wise men who advise them. Unchecked gods, fallen angels, can still oppress and corrupt the creation.

The Son of Man in the Book of Enoch

What or Who exactly was the Son of Man? In later Christian usage, the terms 'Son of Man' and 'Son of God' stood for the human and divine aspects of Jesus, respectively; Son of Man was the human aspect, and the Son of God was divine. However, in the Similitudes of Enoch, the name Son of Man clearly refers to a heavenly figure rather than a human being. This is the first Son of Man problem: which meaning did the gospel writers intend? The second issue is whether the phrase originally referred to Jesus or not. Son of Man does refer to Jesus in the Gospels as we now have them.

But was this a later development of Christian thinking, and not a part of Jesus' own description of himself? In some of the sayings it could conceivably be referring to someone else. For example, in Mark 14.61-62 the High Priest asks: 'Are you the Christ, the Son of the Blessed?' and Jesus replies: 'I am; and you will see the Son of man seated at the right hand of Power [...]' If we cannot prove that being the Christ, the Son of the Blessed, was the same as being the Son of Man (i.e. if we cannot prove that Son of Man was associated with the Messiah), then it is just possible that Jesus was referring to someone other than himself at the right hand of God. The answer to this question is very important in helping us understand how Jesus saw himself, because the phrase Son of Man is used in the Gospels in the sayings of Jesus, and seems to have been characteristic of him. Did he say these things about himself (i.e. was he the Son of Man), or did he refer to another as Son of Man? And was 'son of man' just the phrase for a human being, as later usage implied, or was it an angelic tide, as Enoch suggests?

It is true that the phrase "Son of Man" can be interpreted in different ways, and there has been a long debate about its meaning in the New Testament. Some argue that the phrase simply means "a man" and was used by Jesus to refer to himself, emphasizing his humanity. Others suggest that it has a more elevated meaning and refers to an angelic or divine figure sent by God.

The use of the article "the" in "the Son of Man" can also have different implications. It could be seen as emphasizing the uniqueness and exclusivity of Jesus as the only Son of Man, or it could be understood as simply a way of referring to him in a particular context.

The argument that the phrase originally came from the Aramaic phrase "bar enash" meaning "son of man" used in everyday speech to mean simply a man, adds weight to the interpretation that Jesus used the phrase to refer to himself in a human sense.

However, there are also passages in the New Testament where the phrase "Son of Man" is associated with divine or angelic attributes, suggesting that it has a more elevated meaning. The interchanging use of "I" and "the Son of Man" in certain passages could be seen as evidence that the two phrases have the same meaning.

Ultimately, the meaning of the phrase "Son of Man" is a matter of interpretation, and it is possible that it had multiple layers of meaning for different audiences and contexts.

There appear to be two main perspectives on the meaning and significance of the phrase "Son of Man" in the New Testament. One school of thought holds that the phrase was simply a figure of speech used to refer to a human being, and that its association with a messianic figure arose later in the early Church. The opposing viewpoint holds that the phrase had special meaning and that Jesus purposefully used it to describe himself as a supernatural figure associated with the judgement.

Those who hold the first view argue that the phrase "Son of Man" was equivalent to the phrase "man" or "son of man" in the Old Testament and that its use in the New Testament was simply a continuation of this pattern. They suggest that the early Christians, after realizing who Jesus was, linked the phrase with the famous "Son of Man" passage in Daniel 7, and used this as a template to fill in details of Jesus as the heavenly judge.

They argue that the variations in the use of the phrase in the Gospels could be attributed to the hazards of oral transmission, and not to the wholesale manufacture of a new theology.

On the other hand, those who hold the second view argue that the phrase "Son of Man" had some special significance, and that Jesus intentionally used it to describe himself as a supernatural figure associated with the judgement. They suggest that Jesus was deliberately associating himself with an angelic emissary of the judgement, and that the variations in the use of the phrase in the Gospels can be attributed to the difficulties of translating Jesus' words into different languages and contexts.

To answer the question of who the Son of Man is, evidence from a variety of sources, including Old Testament texts, Enochic literature, and the Gospels themselves, may be required. While the Simihtudes of Enoch paint a clear picture of a supernatural Son of Man figure, they have not been admitted as evidence in the New Testament debate due to their uncertain dating. However, a thorough examination of all available sources may shed light on the meaning and significance of the phrase "Son of Man" in the New Testament.

If we read Isaiah 1-39 we find that the themes of the prophet are remarkably like those of Enoch. Their thought-worlds were the same. I am not saying that the two books are identical, because they are not, but that their authors used the same mental framework in order to communicate. We have already seen how the call vision in Isaiah 6 is very similar to Enoch's, and how Isaiah 24-7 and Isaiah 33 are very Enochic, with their angels and judgement themes. Isaiah, like Enoch, has no real place for the Moses and Exodus theology, but there is great emphasis on judgement (Isa. 2.12-21 ; 5.13-17; 14; 19; 22; 24-7; 34, etc.), the sin of pride (Isa. 14; 37.23-29), angels of judgement (Isa. 37.36-38), the angel mythology (Isa. 14; 24.21-22) and the restoration of creation (Isa. 35). Isaiah's was the world of the first temple, the world in which the Enochic writings claim to have had their roots.

Those who built the second temple, say the Enochic writings, were impure and apostate. It is curious that all these themes from Isaiah are also prominent in Enoch. 1 Enoch does not quote Isaiah or in any way use the book as a source. It is possible therefore that both 1 Enoch and Isaiah come from the same stratum of Israel's history and theology. The one major theme of Isaiah which is not in the pre-Christian Enoch texts at Qumran is the theme of the royal figure. Isaiah 9 and 1 1 both depict a heavenly royal figure who was wise and divine (9.6), who would rule on the throne of David (9.7)5 and who would establish justice and cosmic harmony (11.3-9). The royal figure in Isaiah, which the Christians took to be a prophetic prediction of Jesus, is exactly like the figure we find in the Similitudes. The Similitudes describe him in much more detail, but the basic royal/angelic figure who brings judgement is the same.

I suggest, therefore, that although there is no proof that the Similitudes are pre-Christian, the judgement theme of the Similitudes is an important part of that earlier theology to which the rest of Enoch bears such a strong resemblance, and which we find as a coherent whole in the First Isaiah. The heavenly judgement figure may have been developed and elaborated by later generations, but it was not actually invented by them, nor was it alien to the Enochic tradition.

The roots of the figure in the Similitudes are as old as the traditions in Isaiah. Second, we know that the pre-Christian parts of Enoch had a peculiar code. We do not know why they had it, but only that they did have it. They described angel figures as men or men in white. This is not an insolated usage, in fact it occurs several times. In I Enoch 87.2 we read that beings like white men came from heaven; they were the archangels. In 1 Enoch 89.36 a sheep became a man, meaning that a human being had achieved angelic status.

In 1 Enoch 90.14,22 the heavenly scribe at the great judgement is a man. Cf. also 1 Enoch 93.4, 5,8, the three cases in the Apocalypse of Weeks where human beings become angelic; they are then described as men.

'Man' in Enoch can refer either to an angel, or to a human being who achieves the heavenly angelic state. Now the debate about 'son of man' has concluded from a study of Aramaic usage that 'son of man' only means man. Thus in Daniel 7 'one like a son of man' is only a human figure. But in Enoch 'men' are archangels. It is therefore likely that an angelic vision in Daniel will have used similar terminology. 'A man' was an angel figure, or one who had become angelic.

The Enochic Book of Dreams, where these 'men' occur most frequendy, was written at about the same time as Daniel, during the crisis which led to the Maccabean revolt. It is unlikely that the meanings in Enoch and Daniel were totally different. The figure in Daniel's vision, the 'man', must have been an angel, but since he went to the throne we may perhaps assume that he was like one of Enoch's human beings who became 'men'.

In other words, the son of man figure was a human being who became divine and was given dominion. Like Enoch, Daniel also has animals; in his vision they are the four fearful beasts who represent the four empires. In Revelation there are also beasts, and son of man figures who are angelic; Revelation 1.13 describes 'one like a son of man', and Revelation 14.14 'a son of man, with a golden crown on his head, and a sharp sickle in his hand'. 'A son of man', or a man, meant an angelic figure. We must not read the biblical apocalypses on their own. i Enoch, and works like it, must fill in the details.

If we use the picture of the Son of Man in Enoch, we have a rough guide as to what was implicit in the New Testament. The Son of Man is the heavenly pattern, the heavenly counterpart to a person on earth who fulfils the same role. Notice that it is a person, not the person. Several people had already been called to this task; Ezekiel was commissioned to announce judgement, as were Enoch and Jesus'. They were deemed angelic figures by virtue of their heavenly role. They had visions.

50

They were agents of God. Thus John 5.27 says God has given Jesus authority to execute judgement because he is Son of Man (there is no 'the' in the Greek), Matthew also shows us the old belief that the anointed king was God's agent; he rephrases several passages, and instead of 'God' writes 'Son of Man'. Thus in Mark 9.1 we have 'the kingdom of God', which is paralleled in Matthew 16.28 by 'the kingdom of the Son of man'. The Son of man was the agent and visible manifestation of God. In the parable of the sheep and the goats, the Son of Man is the king who sits in judgement (Matt. 25.31,34), a sure sign that the Son of Man had royal connections.

The Similitudes contain the most detailed description of what the Son of Man was and did. In the first Similitude, he resides beneath the Lord of Spirits' wings. This is a remembrance of the great royal throne in the temple, which was flanked by cherubim wings. In his days, justice is established; the great judgement is performed in front of him, just as it was in the ancient temple rituals. The Elect One will sit on the throne of judgement, the earth will be transformed, and the elect ones will live there, according to the second Similitude.

The Son of Man approaches the Ancient of Days, and the angel reveals that he will be the judge of kings and the powerful. The words are similar to the Magnificat. What could have sparked the inspiration for this ancient Christian canticle? A similar standard of judgement? Why was it given to Mary? If it was truly associated with her or the expectations of people of her background, was an Enochic expectation of judgement part of Jesus' upbringing? These are all speculative questions, but they are meant to make us think.

THE BOOK OF ENOCH

Chapter one

The words of Enoch's blessing, bestowed on the elect and righteous who will endure the day of tribulation, when all the wicked and godless will be destroyed.

Enoch, a righteous man whose eyes were opened by God, began his account with these words, describing how he saw a vision of the Holy One in heaven, which the angels revealed to him, and he heard everything they said, saw, and understood, despite the fact that it was not meant for his generation, but for a distant future generation.

Regarding the elect, he said, "The Holy Great One will come forth from His dwelling,"
The eternal God will tread upon the earth, even Mount Sinai, and appear in the fullness of His power from heaven."
"And all will tremble with fear, the Watchers will quake, and great terror and trembling will grip them to the ends of the earth."
"The high mountains will shake, and the tall hills will be brought low and will dissolve like wax in the fire."
"The earth will be torn apart completely and all that is on it will be destroyed, and there will be a judgment upon all."
"But with the righteous, He will make peace, and He will protect the elect with mercy, and they will belong to God and flourish and be blessed, and the light of God will shine upon them."
"And behold, He comes with ten thousand of His holy ones to pass judgment on all and destroy all the ungodly, and to condemn all flesh for all the wicked acts they have committed and all the harsh words the ungodly sinners have spoken against Him."
"Behold all the wonders in the sky, how the celestial lights maintain their set courses and how the luminaries in heaven rise and set in perfect sequence according to their appointed times."

"Examine the earth and understand all the events that take place there, how steadfast they are and how nothing changes, but all the works of God are revealed to you."

"Likewise, the seas and rivers follow their predetermined paths without deviation, due to His commands."

"Consider how the earth is filled with water, clouds, dew, and rain during the summer and winter seasons. During the winter, all of the trees appear to have withered and lost their leaves, with the exception of fourteen trees, which retain their old leaves for two to three years before new ones appear. Consider how the sun shines on the earth during the summer, causing you to seek shade and relief from the heat. Watch as the trees sprout green leaves and bear fruit, knowing that He who lives forever created it this way for you."

"All of God's works are presented to Him year after year, unchanged and completed without change."

"However, you have failed to follow and obey the Lord's commands. Instead, you have turned away and spoken haughty and disrespectful words with your impure mouths against His greatness. Oh, you hard-hearted ones, you shall find no peace. Therefore, you will curse your days and your years of life will wither away, multiplied by an eternal curse, and you shall find no mercy."

"In those days, you will make your names a curse forever to all the righteous, and by you all who curse shall curse, and all the sinners and godless shall curse you forever. And for you, the godless, there shall be a curse."

"The elect, on the other hand, will rejoice and be forgiven of their sins, as well as receive mercy, peace, forbearance, and joy."

"They will discover salvation and light, and they will inherit the earth. The elect will be granted wisdom, and they will live without sinning, whether through forgetfulness or pride. Those who are given wisdom must be humble."

"They will not sin for the rest of their lives, nor will they perish as a result of God's wrath. They will live their entire lives in peace and joy, with increased years of eternal gladness and peace throughout all of their days."

Chapters 6 - 10

And it came to pass that as the population of humanity grew, beautiful and fair daughters were born to them. The angels of heaven, the sons of God, saw these daughters and were drawn to their beauty. They spoke amongst themselves and said, "Let us choose wives from among the children of men and have children with them." Their leader, Semjaza, feared that they may not agree to the plan and that he alone would have to bear the consequences of the great sin. However, they all agreed and swore an oath to follow through with their plan, binding themselves with mutual curses. There were two hundred of them in total, who descended to the summit of Mount Hermon, which was later named after their oath. Their leaders were Samlazaz, Araklba, Rameel, Kokablel, Tamlel, Ramlel, Danel, Ezeqeel, Baraqijal, Asael, Armaros, Batarel, Ananel, Zaqiel, Samsapeel, Satarel, Turel, Jomjael, and Sariel.

The angels took wives, each choosing one, and began having sexual relations with them. They also taught them charms, spells, and plant and root knowledge. The women became pregnant and gave birth to enormous giants. The giants devoured all of man's work and then turned against them. They also started to sin against birds, beasts, and reptiles, as well as each other. The earth was suffused with blood and unjustness.

Azazel taught humanity how to make weapons, jewelry, metal, and precious stonework. People became impious, abandoned God, and committed fornication.

Semjaza taught spells and root-cuttings, Armaros taught counter-spells, Baraqijal taught astrology, Kokabel taught constellations, Ezeqeel taught cloud knowledge, Araqiel taught earth signs, Shamsiel taught sun signs, and Sariel taught moon course. As humanity died, their cries were heard in heaven.

From heaven, Michael, Uriel, Raphael, and Gabriel saw the bloodshed and lawlessness on Earth. The souls of the dead cried out to heaven, making petitions and lamenting their unjust fate. The angels addressed the Lord of all ages, saying, "Nothing can hide from you because you see everything.

Consider Azazel, who has taught all unrighteousness on earth and revealed the eternal secrets of heaven. Semjaza, who taught spells, has had sex with the daughters of men on Earth, revealing all manner of sin." The entire earth was filled with blood and unrighteousness, and the souls of the dead couldn't stop weeping. The Lord knew all things before they happened but said nothing about these things.

Chapters 11 - 15

"And in those days, the storehouse of blessings in heaven will be opened, and blessings will be poured out on the earth and over the children of men's work and labor. Truth and peace will be one throughout the world's days and across all generations of men."

Enoch vanished, and no one of the children of men knew where he was. His involvement was with the Holy Ones and the Watchers. Enoch blessed the Lord of Majesty and the King of the Ages, and the Watchers referred to him as Enoch the Scribe and instructed him to go and inform the Watchers of heaven who had left the high heaven and defiled themselves with women.

"The Watchers have done great destruction on the earth and shall have no peace or forgiveness of sin, as they delight in their children. They shall see the murder of their beloved ones and the destruction of their children and shall lament and make supplication forever but shall receive neither mercy nor peace."

Enoch went and spoke to Azazel and told him that he shall have no peace and a severe sentence has been passed against him. Azazel shall not have rest or mercy because of the unrighteousness which he taught and the works of godlessness.
Enoch spoke to all the Watchers, who were all afraid and seized by fear and trembling. They asked Enoch to write a petition for them so they might find forgiveness, but they were forbidden to speak with the Lord of heaven or lift their eyes to heaven for shame of their sins.

Enoch wrote out their petition and the prayer in regard to their spirits and deeds and requests for forgiveness and forbearance. Enoch sat at the waters of Dan, read their petition until he fell asleep and had a dream of their chastisement. Enoch awoke and went to the Watchers, who were all sitting together and weeping. Enoch told them all the visions he had seen and spoke words of righteousness, reprimanding the Watchers.

This is the book of the words of righteousness and the reprimand of the eternal Watchers according to the Holy Great One's command. Enoch will now speak with a flesh tongue and the breath of his mouth, which the Great One has given to men to speak and understand with their hearts. As the Great One created and gave man the ability to understand the word of wisdom, He created Enoch and gave him the ability to reprimand the Watchers, the children of heaven.

Enoch wrote out the petition of the Watchers, but in his vision, it appeared that their petition will not be granted to them throughout all the days of eternity and that judgment has been finally passed on them. They shall not ascend into heaven again for all eternity and will be bound on earth for all eternity. They will see the destruction of their beloved sons and will have no pleasure in them, as they shall fall before them by the sword.

Enoch saw a vision of clouds inviting and summoning him into a mist, and the course of the stars and flashes of lightning hurried and drove him, and the winds caused him to fly, lifted him up, and bore him into heaven. Enoch entered and was terrified to see a wall made of crystals and surrounded by tongues of fire.

The sky was as clear as water, and a raging fire surrounded the walls and blazed through the doors. Enoch entered the house, which was as hot as fire and as cold as ice, with no pleasure or life, only fear.

"And they took me to a place where the beings were as hot as fire. They could disguise themselves as men whenever they wanted. They led me to a place of darkness and a mountain whose peak reached the heavens. I saw illuminated places, star treasures, and thunder, as well as the depths where a fiery bow, arrows, quiver, sword, and lightning were hidden. They then led me to the waters of life and the fire in the west, which marks the sun's setting.

I came upon a river of fire, where the fire flowed like water into the great sea towards the west. I saw the great rivers and encountered the great darkness and went to a place where no flesh walked. I saw the mountains of the darkness of winter and the source of all the waters of the deep. I saw the mouths of all the rivers on earth and the mouth of the deep.

In my vision, I saw the storehouse of all the winds and how they were beautifully adorned throughout the creation and the solid foundations of the earth. I saw the cornerstone of the earth and the four winds that supported it and the firmament of heaven. I saw how the winds stretch out the height of heaven, stationed between heaven and earth, which were the pillars of heaven. I saw the winds of heaven that turn, bringing the sky, sun, and all the stars to their setting place.

I also saw the winds on Earth carrying the clouds and angels' paths. I saw the firmament of the heaven above at the end of the earth. I continued south and came across a place that burned at all hours of the day and night, with seven mountains of magnificent stones - three to the east and three to the south. The ones to the east were made of colored stone, one of pearl, one of jacinth, and one of red stone. But the middle one, like God's throne, reached to heaven and was made of alabaster, with a sapphire summit.

I saw a great abyss of the earth with pillars of heavenly fire, and I saw among them fiery pillars of heaven, which were falling. Their height and depth were immeasurable, but the place was desert and horrible. I saw there seven stars like great burning mountains, and an angel asked me about them. The angel said, "This place is the end of heaven and earth and has become a prison for the stars and the host of heaven.

The stars that roll over the fire are those that transgressed the commandment of the Lord at the beginning of their rising because they did not come out at their proper times. And He was angry with them and bound them until the time when their guilt is consummated even for ten thousand years."

Uriel, one of the holy angels in charge of the world, turmoil, and terror, told me that the angels who had sex with women would stand there, and their spirits, in various forms, would lead mankind astray into sacrificing to demons as gods. They would remain there until the great judgment when they would be judged and destroyed. Angelic women who went astray would also become sirens.

I, Enoch, was the only one who saw the vision of all things, and no one else will see what I saw. Uriel, Raphael, Raguel, Michael, Saraqael, Gabriel, and Remiel are the names of the holy angels who keep watch."

Chapters 21 - 25

Continuing with the theme, the narrative goes on to describe various other places Enoch encounters as he is taken on a journey by the angels. Each place holds different significance and has its own unique features.

In one place, Enoch sees seven stars of heaven bound in a chaotic and horrible place. When he asks why they are there, one of the angels, Vriel, explains that they are some of the stars that have transgressed the commandment of the Lord and are being punished for their sins.
In another place, Enoch sees a great fire that burns and blazes, and the place is full of falling columns of fire. This, Vriel explains, is the prison of the angels where they will be held forever.

Enoch also sees a mountain range of fire that burns day and night, and seven magnificent mountains with unique stones and beauty beyond it. Enoch is particularly captivated by a tree with a fragrance beyond all fragrances and a fruit that resembles palm dates. When Enoch questions Michael, one of the angels, about the tree, Michael questions why Enoch wants to know the truth.
Throughout his journey, Enoch is amazed by what he sees and learns, but he also feels fear and uncertainty in some of the places he visits. The journey teaches about the consequences of sin and the strength of the Lord's justice.

Chapter 26-30

"And all the valleys were deep and narrow, being formed from hard rock, and there were no trees planted on them.

And I was very amazed at the rocks in the valleys.

And I went from there to the center of the earth, where I saw a blessed place with trees with branches alive and blooming on a cut-down tree.

And there I saw a holy mountain, and beneath the mountain, to the east, was a stream that flowed southward. And I saw another mountain higher than this one to the east, with a deep and narrow valley between them.

It contained a stream that ran beneath the mountain. And to the west of it was another mountain, lower and of lower elevation than the former, with a dry, deep valley between them; another deep and dry valley was at the edge of the three mountains.

What is the purpose of this blessed land, which is entirely covered with trees, and what is the purpose of this cursed valley between them?' I asked.

Then Vriel, one of the holy angels with me, replied, 'This accursed valley is for those who are cursed forever: Here shall all the accursed be gathered together who utter with their lips words against the Lord not befitting His glory or say hard things against Him. They will be gathered here, and this will be their place of judgment.

There will be a spectacle of righteous judgment on them in the presence of the righteous forever in the last days: here will the merciful bless the Lord of glory, the Eternal.

Then, I went towards the east, into the midst of the mountain range in the desert, and I saw a wilderness.

And it was solitary, full of trees and plants. And water gushed out from above.

Rushing like a torrent that flowed towards the northwest it caused clouds and dew to fall on every side.

Then I went to another location in the desert and approached the mountain range to the east.

And there I saw aromatic trees exuding the fragrance of frankincense and myrrh, trees that looked similar to almond trees.

Beyond these, I went to the east and saw another place, a valley full of water that never ran dry.

And there was a fragrant tree, the color of which was mastic. And I noticed fragrant cinnamon on the sides of those valleys. I continued eastward after these."

Chapters 31 - 35

"And I saw other mountains, and among them were groves of trees, and there was nectar that flowed from them, which is named Sarara and Galbanum.

And beyond these mountains, I saw another mountain to the east of the ends of the earth, on which there were aloe trees, and all the trees were full of fruit, being like almond trees.

And when it was burned it smelled sweeter than any fragrant odor.

And after I had smelled these fragrant odors, I looked towards the north over the mountains and saw mountains full of fine nard and fragrant trees of cinnamon and pepper.

And then I passed over the summits of all these mountains, far to the east of the earth, and passed over the Red Sea, and then passed over the angel Zotiel.

I arrived at the Garden of Righteousness. Beyond those trees, I noticed more trees, which were numerous and large. There were two very large, beautiful, glorious, and magnificent trees there. They ate the holy fruit of the tree of knowledge and gained great wisdom.

That tree has the height of a fir, the leaves of a Carob tree, and the fruit is like grape clusters, very beautiful: and the fragrance of the tree travels far.

And from there I went to the ends of the earth and saw there large beasts, and each differed from the other; and I saw birds also differing in appearance and beauty and voice, the one differing from the other."

"And to the east of those beasts I saw the ends of the earth where heaven rests on it, and the doors of heaven open. And I saw how the stars of heaven come out, and I counted the gates from which they came out, and wrote down all their outlets, of each individual star by their number and their names, their courses and their positions, and their times and their months, as Uriel the holy angel who was with me showed me.

He showed me all things and wrote them down for me; also their names he wrote for me, and their laws and their functions.

From there I went towards the north to the ends of the earth, and there I saw a great and glorious device at the ends of the whole earth."

"And here I saw three gates of heaven open, through which north winds blow, bringing cold, hail, frost, snow, dew, and rain.

And they blow for good through one gate, but for violence and torment on the earth through the other two gates, and they blow with force.

Then I went west to the ends of the earth and saw three gates of heaven open, just as I had seen in the east, with the same number of gates and outlets."

Chapters 36 - 40

"So I travelled to the earth's southernmost reaches and saw three open gates of heaven, from which dew, rain, and wind flowed.

Then I went to the eastern limits of heaven, where I saw the three eastern gates of heaven open, with smaller gates above them. The stars of heaven pass through these smaller gates and follow the path laid out for them to the west.

I always blessed the Lord of Glory and praised His greatness, as I beheld the wonders He has done and shown to the angels, spirits, and men so that they might give glory to His work and creation, and recognize the power of His might."

The second vision was seen by Enoch, Jared's son, who saw the vision of wisdom and spoke wisdom to those on earth.

"Sinners will be driven from the face of the earth when the righteous gather and sinners are judged for their crimes. The Righteous One will appear in the presence of the elect and righteous, who will be judged by the Lord of spirits. Sinners and those who have denied the Lord of spirits will have no refuge.

The elect and holy children will descend from heaven at that time, and their descendants will be united with the children of men. Enoch was given books of wrath and turmoil for the unrighteous, for whom there will be no mercy.

A whirlwind lifted me from the ground and carried me to the far reaches of heaven, where I saw the resting places of the holy and righteous. I saw an uncountable number of people standing before the Lord of spirits, surrounded by four figures who did not sleep.

These four presences' voices praised the Lord of glory and blessed the Elect One and those who trust in the Lord of spirits. Another voice prayed and interceded for those on earth, while a fourth voice kept the Satans at bay and forbade them from accusing those on earth before the Lord of spirits."

Chapters 41 - 45

"I witnessed a plethora of secrets in the heavens and learned of the kingdom's division, where men's actions are judged. I saw the abodes of the elect and the holy, as well as the punishment of sinners who reject the Lord of spirits' name. The mysteries of lightning, thunder, winds, clouds, and dew were revealed to me. I learned about the origins and movements of these elements, as well as the wind and cloud storage facilities.

I asked about the significance of this and was told that these were the names of the holy who dwell on earth and believe in the Lord of spirits for eternity.

Wisdom was unable to find a home and was eventually granted a residence in the heavens. Wisdom attempted to live among humans but was unable to find a suitable home and returned to its place among the angels. Unrighteousness, on the other hand, spread from its storehouses, finding and dwelling with those it did not seek.

I saw heaven's stars and their obedient response to the one who calls them by name. I saw how their brightness is measured in a fair balance, as well as the role they play in lightning production.

I also witnessed how some stars transform into lightning and are unable to return to their original form. Another revelation was the penalty for those who deny the name of the holy ones' dwelling and the Lord of spirits. These sinners will not ascend to heaven or dwell on Earth, but will instead suffer on the Day of Judgment. On that day, the Elect One will sit on the throne of glory, judge the righteous, and strengthen their souls. The Elect One will then live among them, transforming heaven and earth into eternal blessings and dwelling places for the elect. Sinners and evildoers, on the other hand, will not be permitted to set foot on the transformed earth."

Chapters 46 - 50

"And there I saw One with an ancient face. His head was white as wool, and He was accompanied by another being whose countenance resembled that of a man, and whose face was full of graciousness, like one of the holy angels.

And I asked the angel who accompanied me and revealed all the hidden things about that Son of Man, who he was, where he came from, and why he went with the Ancient One? And he responded by saying to me:

"This is the son of Man who has righteousness, with whom dwells righteousness, and who reveals all the treasures of that which is hidden, because the Lord of spirits has chosen him, and whose lot has preeminence before the Lord of spirits in righteousness and is for ever. "

And in that place, I saw an unending spring of righteousness. There were many springs of wisdom all around it. And all who were thirsty drank of them and were filled with wisdom, and they lived among the righteous, holy, and elect.

And the Son of Man was named in the presence of the Lord of spirits at that hour, and his name was brought before the Head of Days.

His name was named before the Lord of spirits even before the sun and the signs were created, before the stars of heaven were created.

He shall be a staff to the righteous and they shall steady themselves and not fall. And he shall be the light of the Gentiles, and the hope of those who are troubled of heart.

All who dwell on the earth shall fall down and worship before him and will praise and bless and sing and celebrate the Lord of spirits.

For wisdom is poured out like water, and glory will not fail before him ever. For he is mighty in all the secrets of righteousness, and unrighteousness shall disappear like a shadow, and will no longer exist; because the Elect One stands before the Lord of spirits, and his glory is forever and ever, and his might for all generations.

In him dwells the spirit of wisdom, and the spirit which gives insight, and the spirit of understanding and of might, and the spirit of those who have fallen asleep in righteousness.

And he will judge the secret things, and no one will be able to speak a lie or idle word in his presence, because he is the Elect One before the Lord of spirits, according to His good pleasure.

And in those days, for the holy and elect, a change will occur, and the light of days will abide on them, and glory and honor will return to the Holy.

Affliction will be heaped on the evil on the day of trouble. And in the name of the Lord of spirits, the righteous will triumph. For He will do this to others in order for them to repent and turn away from their works.

They shall have no honor through the name of the Lord of spirits, but through His name, they shall be saved, and the Lord of spirits will have compassion on them, for His mercy is great."

Chapters 51 - 55

"The earth will return what has been entrusted to it during those days, and the grave will release what it has received. Hell will repay its debts because the Elect One will appear. He will select the righteous and holy from among them and bring salvation to them. The Elect One will sit on His throne, and His mouth will be filled with wisdom and counsel. These gifts have been given and glorified by the Lord of Spirits.

Mountains will leap like rams, hills will skip like lambs, and all the angels in heaven will rejoice. The earth will rejoice, and the righteous will dwell on it. After those days, I was carried off in a whirlwind and brought to the west, where I saw all the secret things of heaven. I saw mountains of iron, copper, silver, gold, soft metal, and lead. I asked the angel who accompanied me what these things were, and he told me they would serve the authority of the Messiah, so that He may be powerful and mighty on the earth.

Michael, Gabriel, Raphael, and Phanuel will take hold of them on that great day and throw them into the burning furnace. The Lord of spirits will take vengeance on them for their unrighteousness and for leading those on earth astray.

The angel of peace told me that if I waited a little longer, all secrets would be revealed. I saw a deep valley with its mouth open, into which all those from the earth, sea, and islands would bring gifts and tokens of homage, but the valley would never be filled. Sinners will destroy the work of the righteous and will be destroyed in the presence of the Lord of spirits, banished from the face of the earth, and perished forever.

The angels of punishment were seen preparing instruments for the earth's kings and were powerful to destroy them as well. They forged immeasurable iron chains and prepared them for Azazel's hosts.

The Lord of spirits swore by His great name that He would never do this again and set a sign in heaven, making a covenant of good faith between Him and those on earth for as long as heaven is above the earth, according to His command."

Chapters 56 - 60

"In those days the angels shall return and gather together and throw themselves to the east on the Parthians and Medes. They shall stir up the kings, so that a spirit of unrest and disturbance will come on them, and they shall drive them from their thrones, that they may rush out like lions from their lairs, and as hungry wolves among their flocks.

And it came to pass after this that I saw another host of chariots, and men riding on them. They were coming on the winds from the east, and from the west to the south.

The noise of their chariots was heard, and when this turmoil took place the holy ones from heaven watched it, and the pillars of the earth were shaken and moved, and the sound of it was heard from the one end of heaven to the other, in one day.

And all shall fall down and worship the Lord of spirits. This is the end of the second Parable.

And I began to speak the third Parable concerning the righteous and elect. Blessed are you, you righteous and elect, for glorious shall be your lot.

And the righteous shall be in the light of the sun, and the elect will be in the light of eternal life. The days of their life shall be unending, and the days of the holy will be without number.

And they shall seek the light and find righteousness with the Lord of spirits. Peace to the righteous in the name of the Eternal Lord!

My eyes saw the secrets of the lightning and the lights in those days, and they judge and execute their judgment, and they illuminate for a blessing or a curse as the Lord of spirits wills.

And there I saw the secrets of thunder, and how when it resounds above in heaven, the sound thereof is heard, and he caused me to see the judgments executed on the earth, whether they are for well-being and blessing, or for a curse, according to the Lord of spirits' word.

After that, I was shown all the secrets of the lights and lightning, and they lighten for blessing and satisfaction.

In the year 500, on the fourteenth day of the seventh month of Enoch's life, I saw in that parable how a mighty quaking caused the heaven of heavens to quake, and the host of the Most High, and the angels, a thousand thousands and ten thousand times ten thousand, were disquieted with great foreboding.

And the Head of Days sat on the throne of His glory, surrounded by angels and the righteous.

And a great tremor gripped me, and fear gripped me, and my legs buckled, and I melted with weakness and fell on my face."

Chapters 61 - 65

"Angels were given long cords and flew northward with wings back then. When I asked one of the angels why they had taken flight, he said it was to take measurements. The angel who accompanied me said that these measurements would bring righteousness to the righteous and cords to the righteous, allowing them to rely on the Lord of spirits for eternity. The elect would then live with the elect, and these measurements would strengthen their faith.

These measurements would also reveal all the secrets hidden in the depths of the earth, including those who had been destroyed, devoured by beasts, or consumed by sea creatures, so they may return and rely on the day of the Elect One. None can be destroyed before the Lord of spirits.

The Lord commanded kings, the powerful, the exalted, and all those who dwell on the earth to open their eyes and recognize the Elect One. He was seated on the throne of glory by the Lord of spirits, and righteousness was poured out on Him. All sinners are destroyed by His word, and all unrighteousness is eradicated in His presence. All kings, the mighty, the exalted, and all who hold the earth will stand up and acknowledge that He sits on the throne of glory, and righteousness is judged before Him, with no lying word spoken. Every secret will be revealed, and His power will be passed down from generation to generation, with His glory lasting forever.

However, those who have not believed in Him, nor glorified the name of the Lord of spirits, but have put their hope in their kingdom and glory, will be driven away and will find no respite. Light will vanish from their presence, and darkness will be their dwelling place for eternity.

When Noah realized that the earth was sinking and that its destruction was imminent, he went to the ends of the earth and cried out to his grandfather Enoch. With a bitter voice, Enoch approached him and asked why he was crying.

The Lord had issued a command that those who dwell on the earth would face ruin because they had discovered all the secrets of the angels and all the violence of the deceivers. This included all of the powers possessed by those who practiced sorcery, and witchcraft, and created molten images for the entire earth.

Chapters 66 - 70

"And the Lord revealed to me the angels of punishment, ready to unleash the full power of the waters beneath the earth, in order to bring judgment and destruction upon all those who inhabit the earth. The Lord of spirits commanded the departing angels not to raise the waters, but to control them, as they were responsible for the forces of the waters. I left the presence of Enoch.

'Noah, your lot is before me, blameless and filled with love and righteousness,' the word of God came to me. The angels are building a wooden structure, and when they're done, I'll place my hand on it to protect it. The seed of life will emerge from it, and the earth will no longer be devoid of inhabitants. I will always remember your seed, and I will spread those who dwell with you. The earth's surface will become fruitful, and they will be blessed and multiply on the earth in the Lord's name.'

He will imprison the unrighteous angels in the burning valley that my grandfather Enoch showed me in the mountains of gold, silver, iron, and other metals in the west. After that, my grandfather Enoch shared with me the secrets contained in the book of Parables, which he had collected for me.

'The power of the spirit grips me and makes me tremble because of the severity of the judgment of the secrets and the judgment of the angels,' Michael said to Raphael on that day. Who can withstand the intense judgment that has been delivered, causing them to melt away?' "Who would not have a softened heart about this, and whose mind would not be troubled by this judgment against them because of those who have led them astray?" Michael responded.

When Michael stood before the Lord of spirits, he said to Raphael: 'I will not defend them in the presence of the Lord, for the Lord of spirits is angry with them for acting as if they were the Lord. And after this judgment, I will terrify them and make them tremble for showing this to those who dwell on the earth.'

The names of those angels are as follows: Samjaza, Artaqifa, Armen, Kokabe, Turael, Rumjal, Danjal, NeqaeI, Baraqel, Azazel, Armaros, Batarjal, Busasejal, Hananel, Turel, Simapesiel, Jetrel, Tumael, Turel, Rumjal, and Azazyel. These are their leaders' names, as well as the names of their leaders by the hundreds, fifties, and tens. The first of these is Jeqon, who led God's sons astray and brought them down to earth via the daughters of men.

And it came to pass during his lifetime that his name was elevated to Son of Man and Lord of spirits among those who dwell on earth. He was lifted up on the spirit chariots, and his name vanished among them. I was no longer one of them as of that day. He positioned me between the two winds, between the North and West, where the angels measured the place for the elect and righteous. And there I saw the first fathers and the righteous who had lived there since the beginning."

"And it happened that my spirit was carried away and ascended into heaven, where I saw the holy angels' sons, the sons of God. They were walking on fire, their clothes white and their faces white as snow.

I fell on my face before the Lord of spirits after seeing two rivers of fire, their light shining like hyacinth. Michael, the archangel, took my hand, lifted me up, and led me to all the secrets of righteousness. He revealed to me all the secrets of the ends of heaven, the star stores, and all the lights that proceed before the holy ones.

The book of the courses of the luminaries of heaven, the relations of each according to their name, origin, and months of dominion and seasons, was shown to me by Uriel, the holy angel who was my guide. He showed me all their laws and regulations exactly as they are, and how it is with each of the years of the world and to eternity, until the new creation is accomplished which endures forever.

The first luminary law states that the Sun rises in the eastern gates of heaven and sets in the western gates. I saw six doors through which the Sun rises and six doors through which it sets, and the Moon rises and sets in these doors, and the stars and those they lead follow each other in corresponding order, six doors in the east and six doors in the west. Many windows were also seen to the right and left of these doors, with the great luminary, the Sun, leading the way, its sphere like the sphere of heaven, filled with illuminating and heating fire.

The second law deals with the Moon, whose orbit is like the sphere of heaven, driven by the wind and given light in measurement. Its rising and setting change every month and its days are like the days of the Sun, with its light full, it is a seventh part of the Sun's light. And thus it rises, its first phase in the east appearing on the thirtieth morning, visible with the Sun in the door where the Sun rises.

Another course I saw was a lunar law and how it performs its monthly revolution. All of this was revealed to me by Uriel, the holy angel who leads them all, and I wrote down their positions and months as they were revealed to me, as well as the appearance of their lights until fifteen days had passed. The Moon completes all of its light in the east and all of its darkness in the west in seven parts. It changes its settings in some months and takes its own strange path in others. The Moon will set with the Sun in the third and fourth middle doors in two months.

The leaders of the heads of the ten thousand, who are in charge of all creation and the stars, also have to do with the four days of the year which are not counted in the yearly calendar, and they render service on these four days. Men go wrong in them because these luminaries truly render service to the stations of the world, one in the first door, one in the third door of heaven, one in the fourth door, and one in the sixth door, with the exactness of the year accomplished through its separate three hundred and sixty-four stations."

Chapters 76- 80

"I saw twelve doors open to all four corners of the heavens in the far reaches of the earth, from which the winds issue forth and blow across the earth. Three doors faced the heavens' front, three faced west, three faced the heavens' right, and three faced the heavens' left. The first three doors were in the east, followed by three in the north, three to the south's left, and three in the west. Four doors released winds that brought blessings and prosperity (peace), while the remaining eight doors released winds that wreaked havoc on the earth, its inhabitants, and everything in the water and on land.

The first wind from these doors, known as the east wind, emerges from the first door in the east and moves south, bringing desolation, drought, heat, and destruction with it. The first quarter is called the east because it is the first, and the second quarter is called the south because the Most High will descend from there. The west quarter is known as the diminished quarter because all celestial luminaries wane and set there. The fourth quarter, the north, is divided into three sections: one for human habitation, one for seas of water, the deep, forests, rivers, darkness, and clouds, and one for the Garden of Righteousness.

I saw seven high mountains that were higher than any other mountains on the planet, where hoar-frost formed and time passed in the form of days, seasons, and years. The sun has two names, Orjares and Tomas, and the moon has four names, Asonja, Ebla, Benase, and Erae. The sun and the moon are two great luminaries, and their spheres are identical in size to the sphere of heaven. The sun's sphere contains seven times as much light as the moon, and it is transferred in fixed measurements until the seventh portion of the sun is depleted.

And now I have shown you everything, my son Methuselah, including the laws of all the stars in heaven. I have revealed to you the laws that govern their daily, seasonal, and yearly movements, as well as their departures and the order assigned to each month and week.

I've also shown you the moon's waning, which occurs in the sixth door and when her light is complete. And the waning that occurs in the first door in its season lasts one hundred and seventy-seven days, or twenty-five weeks and two days in weeks.

"Enoch, behold, I have shown you everything, and I have revealed to you the sun, the moon, and the leaders of the stars in heaven, and all their movements, tasks, and times," the angel Uriel said to me at the time. The years will be shortened during the days of the sinners, and their crops will be late on their lands and fields, causing all things on earth to change and not appear in their proper time. The rain will be held back by the heavens. The earth's fruits will be delayed and will not grow at their proper time, while the trees' fruits will be withheld. The moon will alter her customs and not appear at her proper time. The sun will be seen in the evening on the edge of the great chariot in the west, shining brighter than is normal according to the order of light."

Chapters 81 - 85

'Enoch, look at these heavenly tablets and read what is written on them, and mark every individual fact,' he said.

And I looked at the heavenly tablets, and read everything that was written on them, and understood everything, and read the book of all mankind's deeds, and of all the children of the flesh, which shall be on the earth until the end of generations.

And I exalted the Lord for His patience and blessed Him for the children of men, and I blessed the great Lord, the King of glory forever, for creating all the works of the world (sons of Abraham).

'Blessed is the man who dies in righteousness and goodness, against whom no book of unrighteousness is written, and against whom no day of judgment shall be found,' I said.

And now, my son Methuselah, I'm telling you about it and writing it down for you!

I have given wisdom to you, your children, and future generations, so that they may pass it down for generations. This wisdom is that which transcends their comprehension.

And those who understand it will not sleep but will listen in order to learn this wisdom, and it will satisfy those who eat it better than good food.

And now, my son Methuselah, I will show you all my visions, recounting them in front of you.

I had two visions before I married (took a wife), and one was quite different from the other: the first when I was learning to write, and the second before I married (took) your mother.

And regarding them I prayed to the Lord. I had laid down in the house of my grandfather Mahalalel, when I saw in a vision how heaven collapsed and was carried off (removed, torn down) and fell to the earth.

And when it fell to the earth, I saw how the earth was swallowed up in a great abyss, with mountains suspended on mountains, hills sinking down on hills, and high trees ripped from their stems and hurled down and sunk in the abyss.

And I lifted up my hands in righteousness and blessed the Holy and Great One, and spoke with the breath of my mouth and with the tongue of flesh, which God has made for the children of the flesh of men, that they may speak, and He gave them breath, a tongue, and a mouth, that they may speak:

Blessed are you, Lord, King, Great and Mighty in your Might, Lord of the entire creation of heaven, King of kings, and God of the entire world. And your power, kingship, and greatness endure for all generations, and all heavens are your throne for all time, and the entire earth is your footstool for all time.

And then I had another dream, which I will show you, my son, in its entirety. And Enoch lifted up his voice and spoke to his son Methuselah: 'I will speak to you, my son, hear my words. Pay attention to your father's dream (vision).

Chapters 86 - 90

As I slept again, I had a vision of the sky above. A star fell from heaven and rose up to graze among the oxen.

I then noticed the large and black oxen, and they all changed their stalls and pasturelands, as well as their heifers, and began to coexist.

In my vision, I saw many stars descending and falling from heaven to join the first star, transforming into bulls among the cattle and grazing with them.

I noticed that they all let go of their private parts like horses and began to mate with the bulls' cows. And they all got pregnant and had elephants, camels, and donkeys.

I then saw them gore and devour each other, causing the earth to scream. I raised my eyes to the sky once more, and I saw beings that resembled white men. Four of them appeared from heaven, followed by three others.

The three who had arrived last took my hand in theirs and lifted me above the earth's generations, showing me a tower that was high above the earth and all the hills were below.

One of them said to me, "Stay here until you see everything that happens to the elephants, camels, donkeys, stars, and oxen, and all of them."

I saw one of the four who had arrived first seize the first star that had fallen from heaven and bind it hand and foot before casting it into a horrible and dark abyss. Another drew a sword and handed it to the elephants, camels, and donkeys, who then began to fight each other, causing the entire earth to shake. As I watched in my vision, one of the four who had appeared stoned them from heaven and gathered the great stars with private parts like horses and bound them all, throwing them into the earth's abyss.

One of the four went to the white bull and taught it a secret, and the bull, now a man, built a large vessel and lived in it. Three bulls lived with him on the ship and were completely covered. I returned my gaze to heaven and saw a high roof with seven water torrents flowing into a large enclosure. I watched as fountains opened on the surface of the great enclosure, causing water to rise until it covered the entire surface. The water, darkness, and mist grew, and I saw the water rise above the enclosure's height and stream over it, standing on the earth.

In this manner, thirty-five shepherds took on the task of grazing the sheep, completing their periods one after the other. Others then took over, each in their own period. I then saw all the birds of heaven coming, led by eagles, vultures, kites, and ravens, and they began to devour the sheep, picking out their eyes and eating their flesh.

I watched as the sheep cried out, but their flesh was being consumed by the birds. In my sleep, I mourned for the shepherd who had tended to the sheep. I saw the sheep being devoured by dogs, eagles, and kites, leaving behind only bones. The bones too fell to the earth and the sheep became few.

Chapters 91 - 95

Gather your brothers and all the descendants of your mother, my son Methuselah, to hear what I have to say. The word has come to me, and the spirit is upon me, so that I may reveal everything that is to come to you.

Methuselah did as he was told and summoned his brothers and relatives. He then addressed the righteous children, saying:

"Listen to your father's words, Enoch's sons. Pay attention to what I say because I want you to love and live righteousness, my beloved. Walk in righteousness rather than with those who have a divided heart. It will guide you in the right direction. Righteousness will never abandon you.

I am certain that the earth will be subjected to violence and destruction, and that the earth will be severely punished. Unrighteousness will once again reign supreme, and sin and violence will triumph. However, do not be alarmed by these occurrences. The Holy and Great One has set aside specific days for everything.

Keep my words in your hearts and do not let them be forgotten, for I know that sinners will try to suppress wisdom.

The righteous will rise from their sleep and walk in righteousness, always doing good and living in grace. They will be endowed with goodness and righteousness and receive eternal righteousness. They will walk in eternal light, while sin will perish in eternal darkness.

"I was born in the seventh year of the first week, a time of judgment and righteousness," Enoch began to recount what he had learned from the heavenly books. Wickedness and deception will emerge in the second week, leading to the end. I warn the righteous to stay away from wickedness and death.

Choose righteousness and peace instead, and you will live and thrive.

Woe to those who build their houses on unrighteousness and deceit, for they will be suddenly overthrown and have no peace.

Woe to those who build their houses with sin, for they will be destroyed by the sword. Those who amass wealth in gold and silver will perish suddenly in the judgment.

Sinners who have allowed themselves to commit evil will be judged. Do not be afraid of the sinners, for the Lord will deliver them into your hands for judgment. But woe to those who speak against God, for your sins will keep you from receiving healing. Woe to those who return evil for good, for they will be punished for their actions. Woe to the false witnesses and those who commit injustice, for they will perish suddenly."

Chapters 96 - 100

Be encouraged, you righteous; for sinners will perish suddenly before you, and you will rule over them according to your desires.

And in the day of the sinners' tribulation, your children will mount and rise like eagles, and your nests will be higher than the vultures'. You will ascend as badgers and enter the earth's crevices and rock clefts forever before the unrighteous. Because of you, the satyrs (sirens) will sigh and weep.

So, fear not, you who have suffered, for healing will be your portion, and a bright light will enlighten you, and you will hear the voice of rest from heaven.

Woe to you, you sinners, for your riches make you appear like the righteous, but your hearts convict you of being sinners, and this fact shall be a testimony against you for a memorial of your evil deeds.

Believe, you righteous, that in the day of unrighteousness, sinners will be ashamed and perish.

Be aware, you sinners, that the Most High is mindful of your destruction, and the angels of heaven rejoice over it.

What will you do, you sinners, and where will you flee on the day of judgement, when you hear the voice of righteous prayer?

You will suffer the same fate as them, for whom these words will bear witness: "You have been sinners' companions."

And in those days the prayer of the righteous shall reach to the Lord, and for you the days of your judgment shall come.

And all the words of your unrighteousness shall be read out before the Great Holy One, and your faces shall be covered with shame, and He will reject every work which is grounded on unrighteousness.

And now I swear to you, to the wise and to the foolish, that you shall see many experiences on the earth.

For you men shall put on more adornments than a woman, and colored garments more than a young woman, like royalty and in grandeur and in power, and in silver and in gold and in purple, and in splendor and in the food they shall be poured out as water.

As a result, they will have neither knowledge nor wisdom, and they will perish along with their possessions; and with all their glory and splendor, and in shame and slaughter and great destitution, their spirits will be thrown into the furnace of fire.

I have sworn to you, you sinners, that just as a mountain does not become a slave, and a hill does not become the servant of a woman, so sin was not sent on the earth, but man created it, and those who commit it will face a great curse.

And the woman is not cursed with barrenness, but she dies without children as a result of her own actions.

Prepare, you righteous, to raise your prayers as a memorial and place them as a testimony before the angels, so that they may place the sins of the sinners before the Most High as a reminder.

The nations will be stirred up in those days, and the families of the nations will rise on the day of destruction.

And in those days, the destitute will go and throw their children out, abandoning them, so that their children will perish as a result of them. They will abandon their babies (sucklings) and not return to them, and they will have no pity for their loved ones.

Chapters 101 - 105

They are afraid of the sea and everything it contains because they put their trust in worldly possessions. But isn't the sea and its movements the work of the Most High, who has set limits and bound it with sand? The sea is afraid of His rebuke and dries up, but why are sinners on earth afraid of Him? He created the heavens and the earth, as well as everything in them, including the creatures that move on it and in the sea. Even sailors who brave the depths of the sea fear it, whereas sinners do not fear the Most High.

If He sent a fire to consume them, where would they flee to find safety? Will they not tremble and be afraid when He speaks His Word against them? The stars will tremble, the earth will shake, and all the angels will flee from the presence of God, who is great and glorious, while the children of the earth will tremble and shake. The wicked will be cursed for all eternity and will have no peace. But do not be afraid, righteous souls and those who have died in righteousness, for all good and joy and glory is prepared for them, and they will live and rejoice forever.

The wicked's spirits, on the other hand, will be cursed and die in their sins, without peace or hope. The wise and righteous are called to teach and guide the children of the earth, and they and their wisdom will be forever united in the paths of righteousness with the Most High and His son. Though the wicked may prosper, the righteous must avoid their violence, for they will become companions of the hosts of heaven, and their sins will be recorded on a daily basis. All their sins are visible in light and darkness, day and night, and the Lord calls on the wise and righteous to show the way to peace and righteousness.

Chapters 106 - 108

And after a few days, my son Methuselah took a wife for his son, Lamech, and she became pregnant and bore a son through him. And his body was white as snow and red as a rose in bloom, and his head hair and long curls were white as wool, and his eyes were beautiful.

When he opened his eyes, he lit up the entire house like the sun, and it was very bright.

And on it, he levitated (rose) in the midwife's hands, opened his mouth, and spoke with the Lord of righteousness.

And his father, Lamech, was terrified of him and fled, returning to Methuselah. 'I have begotten a strange son, different and unlike man, and resembling the sons of the God of heaven; and his nature is different and he is not like us, and his eyes are as the rays of the sun, and his face is glorious,' he said to him.

Another book written by Enoch for his son Methuselah and those who will follow him in keeping the law in the last days.

You who have done good will have to wait until those who work evil are destroyed and the power of the wrongdoers is removed.

And wait until sin has passed away, for their names will be blotted out of the book of life and the holy books, and their (children's) seed will be destroyed for all time, and their spirits will be changed, and they will cry and lament in a chaotic desert, and they will be burned in the fire; for there is no earth there.

I saw something there that looked like an invisible cloud; because it was so deep, I couldn't look over it, but I saw a bright flame of fire and things that looked like shining mountains circling and sweeping back and forth.

'What is this bright thing (shining)?' I asked one of the holy angels who was with me. For there was no heaven, only a blazing fire and the voice of weeping and crying and moaning, lamenting, and agony.

And he said to me, 'This place you see is where the spirits of sinners and blasphemers, as well as those who work wickedness, are cast, as well as the spirits of those who pervert everything that the Lord has spoken through the prophets' mouths and even the prophecies' (things that shall be).

For some of them are written and inscribed above in heaven, so that the angels may read them and know what will happen to sinners, and the spirits of the humble, and those who have afflicted their bodies and been repaid by God, and those who have been abused (put to shame) by wicked men:

Who loved God but did not love gold, silver, or any of the good things in the world, but instead subjected their bodies to torture.

Who, from the moment they were born, yearned for nothing earthly, but saw everything as a passing breath and lived accordingly, and the Lord tried them much, and their spirits were found pure, so that they might bless His name.

And I've written down all the blessings that are meant for them. And he has assigned them their reward because they have been discovered to love heaven more than their life in the world, and they blessed Me despite being trodden underfoot by wicked men, experiencing abuse and reviling from them, and being put to shame.

SUMMARY

The Book of Enoch is an ancient Jewish text that dates back to at least the 2nd century BCE and that was considered sacred by early Christians. It is believed to have been written by Enoch, the son of Jared and the father of Methuselah, who is mentioned in the Bible in Genesis, Hebrews, and Jude. The book is divided into five parts, including The Watchers' Book, The Book of Similitudes, The Book of Astronomical Writings, The Book of Dream Visions, and The Book of the Enoch Epistle. Early church authorities such as Justin Martyr, Augustine, Irenaeus, Origin, and Clement of Alexandria all considered the book to be authentic.

However, it was later rejected by the Council of Laodicea in 381 AD and largely disappeared from view. In recent times, fragments of the book have been discovered in the Dead Sea Scrolls and various Ethiopian versions have been found. The Book of Enoch is considered to be a spiritual scientific textbook that offers a divine explanation for the puzzles of life and prepares us for a paradigm change in the physical, psychological, and spiritual aspects of life. According to the text, Enoch was taken up to heaven for 60 days and during that time he wrote 366 books.

The Book of Enoch is a non-canonical text that was considered sacred by early Christians and was widely read and used in the first three centuries after Christ's death. Enoch, the son of Jared, is mentioned multiple times in the Bible in Genesis 5:18-24, Hebrews 11:5, and Jude 1:14-15, with the latter specifically citing Enoch's book. The book can be divided into five parts:

The Watchers' Book, The Book of Similitudes, The Book of Astronomical Writings, The Book of Dream Visions, and The Book of the Enoch Epistle.

Early church authorities such as Justin Martyr, Augustine, Irenaeus, Origin, and Clement of Alexandria all found The Book of Enoch to be authentic and made use of it. Tertullian even went so far as to call it "Holy Scripture." It was also added to the official Ethiopian Church chronology.

However, in 381 AD, the Council of Laodicea rejected and outlawed The Book of Enoch, and gradually it vanished from mainstream Christianity.

In 1773, James Bruce, a prominent explorer, returned from Abyssinia with three Ethiopian versions of the text, sparking renewed interest in the book. Additionally, many parts of the Greek version have been found over time. In Cave 4 of the Dead Sea Scrolls, seven fragments of The Book of Enoch were found in the Aramaic language.

Enoch's book can be considered as a "book of wisdom" or a "code book" that describes a higher, more evolved evolutionary system of universal intelligence and how it relates to the human race. The text explores 64 fields of future research and serves as the foundation for an ongoing study as part of a 30-year human development plan, spanning a broad range of objective scientific confirmations.

The Book of Enoch is not only a spiritual scientific textbook that sets out the problems of the future in poetic science, but also a source of key, parables, and wisdom that explores the puzzles of life and offers a divine explanation as to why we live in the world. Enoch did not "channel" the text but was given it during a direct, face-to-face encounter with two higher-super literate beings.

Enoch lived for 365 years and is considered the father of Methuselah, the grandfather of Lamech and the great-grandfather of Noah. He is prominently mentioned in the fifth chapter of Genesis which includes his complete genealogy. The historical events surrounding the Book of Enoch are many, with Enoch's Secrets being found only in the Slavonic interpretation. It is believed that Enoch's Secrets had a major impact on the New Testament authors and were used to interpret some of the darker passages in the New Testament.

Enoch was taken up to heaven twice, once for 60 days and during this time he wrote 366 books. He was specifically taken up to heaven on the sixth day of the month Zivan, Enoch was born, and lived three hundred and sixty-five years.

He was brought up to heaven on the first day of the month of Tsivan, he abode sixty days in heaven. He wrote all the signs of all the creation which the LORD had made, and wrote three hundred and sixty-six books, and gave them to his sons, and abode on the earth for thirty days, and was taken up again to heaven on the sixth day of the month of Zivan, in the day and in the hour of his birth. This all is written in the Secrets of Enoch, chapter 68, verse 1-3.

Enoch 22:10 states that the Lord called one of his angels, Pravuil, and commanded him to write all of the secrets of creation. Pravuil then wrote down all of the secrets of creation and the Lord gave him the book to give to Enoch.

In Enoch 22:11, it states that the Lord gave Enoch the book and commanded him to read it, and to teach the children of men all of the secrets contained within it. Enoch was also instructed to reveal the secrets of the creation of man, the spirit of man, and the commandments of God.

Enoch 22:12 states that Enoch began to teach the children of men the secrets of the book, and they began to understand the mysteries of God and the creation of the world. Enoch taught them about the spirit of man, the commandments of God, and the secrets of the creation of the world.

Enoch 22:13 states that the children of men began to understand the secrets of the creation of the world, and they began to fear and worship God. They also began to understand the mysteries of God and the secrets of the creation of the world.

Enoch 22:14 states that the children of men began to understand the secrets of the creation of the world, and they began to fear and worship God. They also began to understand the mysteries of God and the secrets of the creation of the world.

Enoch 22:15 states that the children of men began to understand the secrets of the creation of the world, and they began to fear and worship God. They also began to understand the mysteries of God and the secrets of the creation of the world.

It also states that Enoch continued to teach the children of men the secrets of the book and they continued to understand the mysteries of God and the secrets of the creation of the world.

It's worth noting that the Book of Enoch is considered a pseudepigraphic work, meaning that it is attributed to a biblical figure but is not considered part of the canon of scripture. However, it was widely read and respected in early Jewish and Christian communities and is quoted in the New Testament book of Jude.

The text of the book is divided into five sections, known as "parables." The first parable deals with the fall of the watchers, a group of angels who are said to have descended to earth and taken human wives. The second parable focuses on the judgment of these fallen angels and their offspring, known as the giants. The third parable describes the coming of the Messiah and the final judgment. The fourth parable is a vision of the heavenly throne room and the fifth parable describes the creation of the world and the first humans.

One of the most interesting aspects of the Book of Enoch is its description of the fallen angels, who are said to have taught humans a variety of forbidden knowledge, including metallurgy and the use of cosmetics. The book also describes a hierarchy of angels, with different orders and duties assigned to each. This concept of a hierarchical angelic realm is not found in the canonical texts of the Bible, but it is a common belief in Jewish and Christian apocryphal literature.

The Book of Enoch also contains a number of apocalyptic and eschatological passages, describing the end of the world and the final judgment.

These passages have been influential in the development of Christian eschatology and have influenced the beliefs of various groups throughout history, including the early Christian church and the medieval Knights Templar.

Overall, the Book of Enoch is a fascinating and complex work that offers a glimpse into the beliefs and worldview of ancient Jewish and Christian communities. It is also a valuable source for understanding the development of religious ideas and practices throughout history.

The Book Watchers

The Book of Watchers is the first of five sections in the Book of Enoch and tells the story of the "Watchers," a group of angels who descended to Earth and intermarried with human women, resulting in the creation of a race of giants known as the Nephilim. The text also includes an account of the judgment of these angels by God, as well as a revelation of the future punishment of the wicked.

Many scholars believe that the Book of Enoch was written during the intertestamental period, a time when Jewish religious and cultural traditions were evolving. Some scholars believe that the text was written by a Jewish sect known as the Essenes, while others argue that it was written by a group of Jewish mystics known as the Merkabah mystics.

Despite not being included in the Hebrew Bible, the Book of Enoch was highly regarded by early Jewish and Christian communities. It is quoted in the New Testament book of Jude and was considered canonical by some early Christian communities. However, it was later rejected by both Jewish and Christian authorities and is not considered part of the canon of either tradition.

In recent years, there has been renewed interest in the Book of Enoch among scholars and religious communities, with many claiming that it contains valuable insights into the religious and cultural beliefs of ancient Jewish and early Christian communities.

The Story as written

The book begins with Enoch describing his lineage and how he was chosen by God to be a witness to the secrets of heaven. He tells of his vision of the Watchers, angels who have left their proper habitation and taken on human form to marry and have children with human women. God is angry with them for this transgression and decides to punish them by sending them to earth.

Enoch is taken on a tour of the heavens by the angel Uriel. He sees the stars, the sun, and the moon, and is shown the secrets of the calendar and the movements of the celestial bodies. He also sees the spirits of the dead being judged and sent to their final resting places.

Enoch is shown the Garden of Righteousness and the Tree of Life. He is told that those who are righteous will be allowed to partake of the tree and live forever in the presence of God.

Enoch is taken to the fifth heaven, where he sees the throne of God and the angels singing praises to him. He is told that the end of the world is near and that God will soon bring judgment upon the earth.

Enoch is shown the punishment that will be inflicted upon the Watchers and their offspring, the giants. He is told that they will be bound in chains and thrown into the abyss, never to be released.

Enoch is shown the new heaven and earth that will be created after the judgment. He is told that the righteous will live there in peace and happiness forever.

Enoch is taken back to earth and told to warn the people of the coming judgment. He preaches to them, but they do not listen and continue in their wicked ways.

Enoch is taken up to heaven again and shown the fate of the wicked. He is told that they will be cast into a lake of fire and suffer forever.

Enoch is shown the judgment of the fallen angels and the punishment that will be inflicted upon them. He is told that they will be bound in chains and thrown into the abyss, never to be released.

Enoch is shown the restoration of the earth and the new heaven and earth that will be created after the judgment. He is told that the righteous will live there in peace and happiness forever.

Enoch is shown the future history of the world, including the rise and fall of nations and the coming of the Messiah.

Enoch is taken up to heaven for the last time and is told that he will not die, but will be taken to live with God forever.

Enoch gives a final message of warning and encouragement to the people of the world, telling them to repent and believe in God so that they may be saved from the coming judgment.

The book ends with Enoch being taken up to heaven, where he lives forever in the presence of God. It concludes with a blessing and a call to all who read the book to heed the message of repentance and believe in God, so that they too may be saved.

The book of Parables

In the Book of Enoch's Parables, the parables are presented as visions that Enoch receives from God and are meant to convey moral and spiritual teachings. These parables include descriptions of the end of the world, the judgment of the wicked, and the elect who will be saved. The book also includes a section called the "Astronomical Book," which describes the movement of the stars and the structure of the universe.

The Book of Enoch's Parables have had a significant influence on Jewish and Christian apocryphal literature and have been quoted by early Christian writers such as Tertullian and Justin Martyr. The text was also popular among early Christians and was widely read in the early church. However, it was later rejected by mainstream Christianity and is not considered part of the canon of scripture by most Christian denominations.

The text is also important to certain sects of Christianity such as Ethiopian Orthodox Church, which consider it as a canonical text, and also some modern scholars has been studied it as a source of historical and religious information.

Overall, the Book of Enoch's Parables is a significant text that provides a glimpse into the religious and spiritual beliefs of the time in which it was written and has had a lasting impact on Jewish and Christian apocryphal literature.

The Parables as written in Chapter 37 to 55

Chapter 37 begins with Enoch being taken on a journey by the angels, during which he sees various visions of the end of the world and the judgment of the wicked. In this chapter, Enoch is shown the punishment that will be inflicted on the sinners, including those who have corrupted their ways and those who have oppressed the poor.

In chapter 38, Enoch is shown the fate of the giants, who were the offspring of the angels and the daughters of men. These giants are said to have been punished for their wickedness and for corrupting the earth.

Chapter 39 continues the theme of punishment for sin, with Enoch being shown the punishment of the souls of the wicked after death. Enoch is also shown the place of punishment for the souls of the righteous, which is described as a place of rest and peace.

Chapter 40 describes Enoch's vision of the judgment of the souls of the dead, with the righteous being rewarded with eternal life and the wicked being punished with eternal death. Enoch is also shown the place where the souls of the righteous will dwell after the judgment, which is described as a place of joy and light.

In chapter 41, Enoch is shown the future of the world and the coming of the Messiah. Enoch is told that the Messiah will come to save the righteous and destroy the wicked.

Chapter 42 continues the theme of the coming of the Messiah, with Enoch being shown the glory and honor that will be bestowed upon the Messiah when he comes. Enoch is also told that the Messiah will be the one to judge the living and the dead.

Chapter 43 describes Enoch's vision of the kingdom of heaven, which is described as a place of righteousness and peace where the righteous will dwell forever.

Chapter 44 describes Enoch's vision of the end of the world and the final judgment when the wicked will be punished, and the righteous will be rewarded with eternal life. Enoch is also shown the new heavens and the new earth that will be created after the judgment.

In chapter 45, Enoch is shown the fate of the angels who sinned and the punishment that will be inflicted upon them. Enoch is also told that the angels will be judged according to their deeds.

Chapter 46 continues the theme of the punishment of the wicked and the reward of the righteous. Enoch is shown the punishment of the sinners, who will be consumed by fire, and the reward of the righteous, who will dwell in the kingdom of heaven.

Chapter 47 describes Enoch's vision of the future of the world, with the coming of the end of the world and the final judgment. Enoch is also shown the new heavens and the new earth that will be created after the judgment.

Chapter 48 continues the theme of the end of the world and the final judgment, with Enoch being shown the fate of the wicked and the rewards of the righteous. Enoch is also shown the new heavens and the new earth that will be created after the judgment.

In chapter 49, Enoch is shown the coming of the Messiah and the salvation that he will bring to the righteous. Enoch is also told that the Messiah will be the one to judge the living and the dead.

Chapter 50 describes Enoch's vision of the judgment of the souls of the dead, with the righteous being rewarded with eternal life.

Chapter 51 continues the theme of judgment, with Enoch seeing the sinners being punished for their crimes and the righteous being rewarded with eternal life. Enoch also witnesses the coming of the Lord, who will judge the living and the dead.

Chapter 52 describes Enoch's vision of the end of days, when the Lord will come in glory and the earth will be purified of all wickedness. Enoch sees the Lord's holy ones being gathered together and the wicked being consumed by fire. He also sees the Lord's holy ones entering into eternal life, while the wicked are cast into eternal darkness.

Chapter 53 continues the theme of the end of days, with Enoch seeing the Lord's holy ones being gathered together to receive their reward and the wicked being punished for their sins. Enoch also sees the Lord coming in glory to judge the living and the dead.

Chapter 54 describes Enoch's vision of the new heaven and the new earth, where the Lord's holy ones will dwell forever in peace and happiness. Enoch sees the Lord coming in glory to judge the living and the dead, and the wicked being cast into eternal darkness.

Chapter 55 concludes the book of Enoch's parables with Enoch's final words, in which he encourages the reader to walk in the ways of righteousness and to stay away from the ways of wickedness. Enoch also reminds the reader that the Lord will come to judge the living and the dead and that all will receive their just reward. He also encourages to keep the commandments of God and to follow the example of the righteous.

The book of Visions

The Book of Visions tells the story of Enoch's visions of the end of the world and the judgment of the wicked. In chapter 83, Enoch recounts a dream in which he saw the heavens falling to the earth and the world being swallowed up in a great void. His grandfather, Mahalalel, tells him that this is a vision of the secrets of all the sins of the earth and that Enoch should pray to the Lord of heaven to spare the remnant of the earth. In chapter 84, Enoch prays to God to fulfill his prayer and give him a seed on the earth, and not kill all the flesh of man.

Enoch is shown the various heavens, including the first, second, third, and fourth heavens, as well as the garden of righteousness. Enoch is also shown the various inhabitants of the heavens, including angels, stars, and the souls of the righteous. Enoch is also shown the punishment of the wicked, and the fate of those who have rejected God's commandments. Ultimately, Enoch is shown the glory and majesty of God, and is filled with awe and reverence for the Creator.

In chapter 87, Enoch sees the advent of the seven archangels and is taken to a high position and shown a tower above the land. In chapter 88, he sees an angel take hold of the first star that had fallen from heaven and bind it hand and foot and throw it into the abyss. The world quaked as the lions, camels, and asses began to devour each other. In chapter 89, one of the four angels goes to a white bull (Noah) and instructs him in secret without fear and he builds a great vessel (ark) and dwells thereon with three bulls. Enoch also sees a high roof with seven torrents of water flowing into an enclosure.

In chapter 90, Enoch sees thirty-five shepherds undertaking pasturing in this manner, and they severely completing their periods as did the first. The text seems to refer to the end of the world and the judgment of the wicked, with the righteous being saved by God.

Enoch's Book of Admonition

In the Book of Admonition, Enoch is giving advice and warning to his son Methuselah and his family about the future and the importance of righteousness. He speaks of a coming judgment and chastisement from God, and the destruction of unrighteousness and violence. He urges them to walk in the ways of righteousness and not to be troubled by the times to come. He also speaks of the coming of a chosen one who will bring righteousness and a rule for the righteous in all generations. Enoch also reflects on the difficulty of understanding the things of heaven and the limitations of human knowledge and understanding. He urges his daughters to love righteousness and walk in it, as the paths of righteousness are worthy of recognition. Overall the book is emphasizing on the importance of righteousness and the consequences of unrighteousness.

Enoch words-

In ancient times, there were those who lived wicked lives and gloried in deceit. They were warned that they would perish and not have a good life. Those who perverted the language of righteousness and broke the eternal laws were also warned that they would be deceived on earth. It was advised that the faithful should prepare their prayers for a shrine and set them as a testimony before the angels, in order to bring the guilt of the sinners before the Most High. In those days, the nations and families of nations would emerge, and the poor would be forced to abandon their children, resulting in their children's death. Sinners were warned that the sin was prepared for a day of unceasing bloodshed. Those who worshipped idols and unclean spirits were also warned that they would not receive support from them and would be consumed in their wickedness and terror.

However, those who embraced wisdom and recognized it, and walked in the path of righteousness were blessed and would be saved. On the other hand, those who spread evil to their neighbors, did deceitful and false deeds, and caused bitterness on earth were warned of the punishment in Sheol and that they would not have peace. Similarly, those who denied the measure and eternal inheritance of their ancestors, whose souls obeyed idols, were also warned that they would have no rest.

Those who did wickedness, helped oppression, and slew their neighbors were warned of great judgment and that their glory would be cast down and they would be destroyed by the sword. All the saints and righteous would remember their sins.

In ancient times, when the Lord unleashed His fury in the form of a devastating storm, where could one seek refuge and salvation? And when His wrath was unleashed through His Word, did not fear and trepidation grip the hearts of all? Even the brightest stars trembled with great fear and the entire world was thrown into chaos and alarm. The angels carried out their commands, seeking to hide from the gaze of the Divine glory, while the mortals of the earth trembled and shook, damned to eternal suffering and despair. But fear not, holy souls, for justice shall prevail. And do not grieve, if your soul descends into the depths of Sheol in sorrow and your body fails in this life, despite your righteousness.

Instead, await the day of judgment for the guilty and the day of punishment and rebuke. Yet, when the righteous pass on, the sinners scoff and say "We die just as they do, what profit do they gain from their deeds? See, they too die in sorrow and darkness, what more do they have than we do? From now on, we are equal. What will they receive and what will they see for eternity? Behold, they too die and will see no light." Have you observed the end of the righteous, that there is no violence in them until their passing? Nonetheless, they too die and fade away, their souls sinking into tribulation in Sheol.

Though you may feel forsaken in the midst of a raging storm, know that salvation is not far off. When the Word of the Almighty is unleashed against you, do not fear, for it is in these trying moments that the shining lights of heaven will guide you to safety. The angels will carry out their divine commands, and even the most powerful among us will tremble in awe of the great glory.

But fear not, ye holy souls, for in death there is still hope. Do not grieve if your soul descends into the depths of Sheol in sorrow, for the day of judgment for the guilty is fast approaching. The sinners may mock the righteous, saying, "What profit do they reap for their deeds? They die just like us, in grief and darkness." But do not be fooled, for the end of the righteous is far different from that of the wicked.

Though death may come for all, the path of the righteous is one of peace and no violence is found in them until their final breath. But the wicked, though they may flourish in this life, will ultimately be cast into eternal darkness.

So hold fast to your faith and believe in the justice that is to come. Pray for judgment and it will be granted, for all your tribulations will be inflicted upon those who have wronged you. And when the day of judgment arrives, do not fear for you will stand alongside the heavenly hosts, honored and revered for all eternity.

But beware, for the sins of the wicked will not go unnoticed. Though they may try to alter and pervert the words of righteousness, their deceit will be laid bare in the books of truth. And it is the righteous and wise who will receive these books, to become a cause of joy, uprightness, and wisdom. So stay true to your path of righteousness, for in the end it is the righteous who will be honored and celebrated for all eternity.

The passage seems to be warning about the consequences of moral decay and the importance of living a virtuous life.

APOCRYPHAL BOOKS

Introduction

Apocryphal books are a group of texts that are not considered to be part of the accepted canon of scripture in most major Christian denominations. These texts were widely read and respected in the early centuries of Christianity but were ultimately not included in the canon due to various factors, such as concerns over their historical accuracy or theological soundness.

The term "apocryphal" comes from the Greek word "apokryphos," which means "hidden" or "obscure." The apocryphal books were written between approximately 200 BC and 100 AD and include works such as Tobit, Judith, Wisdom of Solomon, Sirach (also known as Ecclesiasticus), First and Second Maccabees, and the stories of Susanna, Bel and the Dragon, and the Prayer of Manasseh. The New Testament apocryphal books include the Gospel of Thomas, the Gospel of Peter, and the Acts of Paul.

While they are not considered to be part of the biblical canon, the apocryphal books have been important to the history of Christianity and continue to be studied by scholars and religious groups today. Some Protestant denominations include some of these books in their Bibles as "Deuterocanonical" books, while the Roman Catholic, Eastern Orthodox, and Ethiopian Orthodox Churches include all of the apocryphal books as part of their canon.

The list of books considered as apocryphal varies depending on religious tradition. In the Catholic and Orthodox Christian traditions, the following books are considered to be part of the Old Testament apocrypha:

1. Tobit
2. Judith
3. Wisdom of Solomon
4. Sirach (also known as Ecclesiasticus)
5. Baruch
6. First and Second Maccabees
7. Additions to the Book of Esther
8. Additions to the Book of Daniel (Susanna, the Prayer of Azariah, and Bel and the Dragon)

Tobit

Tobit, son of Tobit, son of Ananiel, son of Aduel, son of Gabaet of the descendants of Asiel and the tribe of Naphtali, was a righteous and pious man who lived his life according to the ways of truth and righteousness. Throughout his life, he performed many acts of charity and kindness towards his fellow Israelites who had been exiled to the land of Assyria with him. Tobit was a devout follower of God, and he made it a point to set aside a tenth of his produce for the Levite priests who ministered at the Temple in Jerusalem. He also sold a second tenth of his produce and spent the proceeds each year in Jerusalem, as a way to show his devotion to God.

Tobit was a proud Jew and refused to eat the food of the Gentiles, as he remembered God with all his heart and remained true to his faith. He was a successful businessman and had become the buyer of provisions for King Shalmaneser. Tobit was the proud husband of Anna, a member of his family, and the father of Tobias. Despite his success, Tobit never forgot his duty to give to those in need, as he was taught by his late father and grandmother. Tobit gave the first fruits and tithe to the priests, and he also shared his wealth with the poor and the hungry, giving them food and clothing.

During the reign of King Sennacherib, Tobit showed immense courage by secretly burying those who were fleeing Judea and being hunted down by the king. When Sennacherib learned of Tobit's actions, he ordered Tobit to be executed and seized all of his belongings. Tobit was forced to flee in terror, leaving behind his wife and son. But only fifty days later, Sennacherib was assassinated by two of his sons, and Tobit was eventually able to return to Nineveh, thanks to the intervention of his nephew Ahikar, who was appointed by the new king, Esarhaddon, to oversee all of the kingdom's accounts and administration.

Upon his return, Tobit was reunited with his wife and son, and he celebrated with a feast on the sacred festival of Pentecost. Tobit instructed his son to bring a poor man of their brethren to share in the feast, and while he was waiting, Tobias brought back the news of a fellow Israelite who had been strangled and thrown into the marketplace. Tobit mourned the loss of his fellow Israelite and cried out to God in anguish, asking for mercy and forgiveness for his sins and those of his forefathers.

After burying the dead man, Tobit defiled himself and slept by the courtyard wall, not realizing that there were sparrows on the wall. The sparrow droppings landed in his open eyes and formed white films, leaving Tobit blind and in need of medical help. Despite his blindness, Tobit remained a loving and supportive husband and father, and his wife Anna took up work to support the family. When she was paid, she was also given a baby goat, but Tobit, in his righteousness, told her to return the goat to the owners, as it was not right to eat what was stolen.

Despite the challenges he faced, Tobit never lost his faith in God and cried out to Him in sorrow, asking for relief from his suffering and for the truth to be revealed. Tobit's unwavering devotion to God and his faith in His mercy and justice serve as an inspiration to all who seek to live a life of righteousness and devotion.

Judith

During the twelfth year of Nebuchadnezzar's rule, Judith built strong walls around the city of Ecbatana with stones that were three cubits thick and six cubits long. Despite enlisting the help of multiple nations, the people of the surrounding area refused to assist in the war against King Arphaxad and his army. Enraged, Nebuchadnezzar swore to take revenge on those who disobeyed him, including the territories of Cilicia, Damascus, and Syria, as well as all of the inhabitants of Moab, Ammon, and Judea, and all of Egypt, as far as the two seas.

After defeating King Arphaxad and his army in battle, Nebuchadnezzar and his forces returned to Nineveh, where they rested and feasted for 120 days. Holofernes, the general of Nebuchadnezzar's army, led his troops to attack the western territories and warned that anyone who disobeyed the king would face death.

As they marched, Nebuchadnezzar plundered the cities of Put, Lud, and Rassis, as well as all of the Ishmaelites. He set fire to Damascus' fields during the wheat harvest and pillaged their cities, slaughtering all of the young men and Midianites along the way. He also devastated the cities of Sur and Ocina, as well as Sidon and Tyre.

Nebuchadnezzar desecrated sacred groves and destroyed shrines, as he aimed to extinguish all the gods of the world and become the only deity worshipped by all nations. He enslaved the people he conquered, plundered their homes and killed their cattle, and set up garrisons in the hilltop cities.

The Israelites were filled with terror as Holofernes and his army approached, and they feared for both Jerusalem and the Lord's temple. All of Judea's people gathered, and the priests and high priest Joakim donned sackcloth and cried out to God, pleading for their protection. The people encircled the altar and temple, extending their hands to the Lord in prayer.

Holofernes promised that none of his words would fail and warned the Moabites that the Israelites would be burned, their mountains soaked with blood, and that they would die alongside them. Despite this, the Israelites continued to pray and sought the protection of the Lord.

Wisdom of Solomon

The Wisdom of Solomon speaks of the importance of loving righteousness, seeking the Lord with sincerity of heart, and being holy and disciplined in spirit. It warns that God is a witness of one's inner feelings and a hearer of one's tongue, and that justice will not pass by those who say unrighteous things. The text also addresses the erroneous reasoning of those who believe their lives are brief and sorrowful, and that death is the end, and encourages them to enjoy life's pleasures but to not oppress the poor and righteous. However, it states that the hopes of the wicked are like chaff and that the righteous will receive a glorious crown and a lovely diadem from the Lord. Wisdom will not abandon a just man even when he is sold and will deliver him from sin. The text also mentions the consequences of disregarding wisdom, such as being evident in a perpetually smoking wasteland and being a monument to an unbelieving soul.

The book on Wisdom of Solomon stresses the idea that wisdom is a gift from God, and that those who seek it will find it. The wise person is characterized by their humility, discipline, and love for the truth. They will be protected by God and will always be able to stand confidently in the face of danger or persecution. The choice is ours, and we will reap what we sow.

In contrast, those who live wickedly will experience a terrible end. Their sins will catch up with them and they will suffer the consequences of their actions. Their lives will be filled with turmoil, and their end will be characterized by fear and distress.

The Wisdom of Solomon can be summarized in the writings below-

You rulers of the earth, cultivate love for righteousness and think about the Lord with integrity. Seek Him with a sincere heart, for He can be found by those who do not challenge Him and reveals Himself to those who do not doubt Him. Wisdom will not enter a deceptive soul nor reside in a body enslaved by sin.

Perverse thoughts drive people away from God and when His power is tested, it exposes the foolishness of those who doubt Him. A holy and disciplined spirit will avoid deception, escape foolish thinking, and feel shame when unrighteousness approaches. God is aware of one's inner feelings and thoughts and is a listener of their words. Wisdom is a kind spirit that will not forgive a person who speaks blasphemy. The Lord's Spirit fills the world and the One who holds everything together knows all that is said. No one who speaks unrightly will go unnoticed, and justice will not overlook them when it comes to punishing them. A jealous ear hears all things, and whispers are not unheard. An investigation will be made into the plans of the ungodly, and their words will be reported to the Lord, who will then accuse them of their lawless deeds.

People made a mistake by thinking that life was brief and sorrowful, and that death was the end with no chance of return. They believed that they were born by chance and would disappear as if they never existed. They thought that their breath was smoke, and their reasoning was a spark created by their heartbeat. When the spirit is extinguished, the body turns to ashes and disperses like empty air. Their name will be forgotten with time, and no one will remember their actions. Their lives will vanish like mist chased away by the sun's rays. They believed that their time was like a shadow that could not be regained, and death was sealed, with no chance of return. So, they decided to enjoy life, drinking wine and perfumes, and never missing an opportunity to celebrate. They oppressed the poor and righteous and did not spare the widow or consider the elderly. The strong were to rule and their might was to be the law of right. They searched for the righteous man because he opposed their actions and criticized them for breaking the law. They decided to put him to the test, insulting and torturing him to see if he was gentle and patient. They sentenced him to a humiliating death because he claimed to be protected. However, their wicked reasoning led them astray, and they did not understand God's hidden purposes or hope for the wages of holiness or discern the prize for blameless souls. God created man for incorruption and in His own image, but death entered the world through the devil's envy.

The righteous man will stand with confidence in front of those who have wronged him and those who made fun of his efforts. They will be scared when they see him and will be amazed at his unexpected salvation. They will confess their sins to each other, feeling deep anguish and say, "This is the man we once mocked and made fun of — we fools!" They thought his life was a sham and his death was unworthy. Why was he counted among God's sons, and how did he end up among the saints? They realized that they had strayed from the truth, and the sun did not shine on them nor did the light of righteousness. They had enough of lawless and destructive paths, but they never encountered the Lord's way. The hopes of the wicked are like chaff, blown away by the wind. The wicked will not remain, but the righteous will receive a glorious crown and a beautiful diadem from the Lord's hand. The Lord will protect them and iniquity will be powerless against the righteous, because the Lord is their refuge and the Most High is their stronghold. They will not fear harm from any man-made disasters or from any deadly sickness that stalks in darkness; for the Lord will be their light and their protection. They will not fear the sudden panic or the destruction of the wicked, because the Lord will be their strength and their song. He will be their rescuer, and they will look in triumph on those who hate them. They will repay their enemies with complete destruction, and the Lord will acknowledge their merits, granting them long life and happiness.

Things to know about the Apocryphal books:

1. Historical significance: The Apocryphal books have played an important role in the history of the Christian Church. They were widely read and used by early Christians, and their influence can be seen in the works of many early Christian writers.

2. Canonization controversy: The canonization of the Apocryphal books was a contentious issue in the early Church. Some Christian communities accepted them as part of the canon, while others rejected them. This debate continued for several centuries, with the canon being finally established in the 4th and 5th centuries.

3. Content: The Apocryphal books include a variety of texts, such as historical narratives, apocalyptic visions, and stories about the birth, life, and death of Jesus. Some of these books also contain teachings and parables that are similar to those found in the New Testament.

4. Relevance today: Despite not being considered part of the canon by many Christian denominations, the Apocryphal books continue to be of interest to scholars and religious groups. They are seen as valuable historical documents that provide insight into the beliefs and practices of early Christians.

5. Translation: The Apocryphal books have been translated into many different languages and are widely available in modern editions. Some are also included in modern Bibles as part of the Deuterocanonical books.

6. Influence on art and literature: The Apocryphal books have had a lasting impact on Western art and literature. They have inspired works by writers, painters, and musicians, and continue to be a source of inspiration for artists and intellectuals today.

Sirach (Ecclesiasticus)

"Sirach" (also known as "Ecclesiasticus") is a book of the Apocrypha and is considered a work of wisdom literature. It is a collection of proverbs, ethical teachings, and reflections on various topics such as God's justice, the importance of wisdom and understanding, the value of humility and compassion, and the dangers of wealth and pride.

The author of Sirach, Jesus ben Sira, was a Jewish sage who lived in Jerusalem around 200 BCE. He wrote the book in Hebrew, but it was later translated into Greek and included in the Septuagint, the Greek translation of the Hebrew Bible used by early Christians.

In Sirach, Jesus ben Sira emphasizes the importance of following the laws and commandments of God, seeking wisdom, and living a righteous and virtuous life. He encourages his readers to be compassionate, kind, and to live in peace with their neighbors. He also speaks out against the dangers of wealth, pride, and the desire for power, warning that these can lead to corruption and sin.

Overall, Sirach is a valuable source of wisdom and moral guidance, offering timeless insights and reflections on the meaning and purpose of life, the nature of God, and the importance of following a virtuous path.

Sirach says that the fear of the Lord is the beginning of wisdom, and it leads to long life. Wisdom was created before all things, and prudence and understanding were present at the creation of the world. No one has access to the source of wisdom but the Lord himself, who saw it and granted it to his works. Wisdom is a gift to those who love the Lord, and it is accompanied by glory, exultation, gladness, and a crown of rejoicing. To have wisdom, one must keep the commandments of the Lord, and those who fear the Lord will receive it as a reward. The Lord is compassionate and merciful, and he rescues those who are in need. Those who fear the Lord will obey his commands and love him, and they will be filled with the law and seek his approval.

Honoring one's father and mother is important, for it brings blessings and atones for sins. Children should help their fathers in old age, even if they lack understanding, and they should not interfere in matters beyond their responsibilities. A man's glory comes from honoring his father and respecting his mother, and a father's blessing strengthens the foundations of a child's home, while a mother's curse can uproot it. A stubborn mind will bring troubles and lead to sin, and a proud person's afflictions will have no cure. The wise man ponders parables and desires to have an attentive ear.

Wisdom and the fear of the Lord lead to long life, blessings, and mercy. One should keep the commandments of the Lord, honor one's parents, and avoid meddling in matters beyond their responsibilities.

Baruch

The Book of Baruch is one of the apocryphal/deuterocanonical books of the Old Testament. It is believed to have been written by Baruch, the secretary of the prophet Jeremiah, around the 5th century BCE. The book primarily deals with the themes of hope, repentance, and the restoration of the Jewish people after the Babylonian exile. It also contains prayers and hymns of praise to God. In addition, it addresses the issue of the divine punishment of the Jewish people for their sins and the restoration of Jerusalem and the Temple. The book also reflects on the Babylonian captivity and the importance of divine wisdom.

The book was widely accepted as scripture by early Jewish communities and was included in the Septuagint, the Greek translation of the Hebrew Bible. However, its canonicity was later questioned by some Christians, and it was eventually excluded from the Protestant Old Testament. Nevertheless, the book remains an important text for both Catholic and Orthodox Christians.

"Baruch" is a book that focuses on the themes of repentance, wisdom, and the sovereignty of God. It is a valuable source of insight into the religious and philosophical beliefs of the Jewish people during the Second Temple period and offers a message of hope and comfort to those facing difficult circumstances.

The story narrated in Baruch:

Baruch the son of Neraiah, a scribe in Babylon, wrote a book during the fifth year of the Babylonian exile. The book was written on the seventh day of the month, at a time when the Chaldeans had taken Jerusalem and burned it to the ground. Baruch read the book to King Jeconiah, the son of Jehoiakim, and to all the people who gathered to hear it, including the mighty men, princes, elders, and people of Babylon who lived by the river Sud. The people wept, fasted, and prayed to the Lord upon hearing the book, and they collected money from each person to send to the high priest Jehoiakim in Jerusalem. At the same time, Baruch returned the silver vessels that King Zedekiah had made to Judah on the tenth of Sivan.

In the book, Baruch spoke of the disobedience and negligence of the people of Israel and Judah towards the Lord their God. The curse and calamities that the Lord had declared through Moses after bringing the forefathers out of Egypt still plagued them to this day. The people had not listened to the Lord's voice in the words of the prophets, but instead followed their own wicked desires and served other gods, resulting in the Lord confirming his word against them. The Lord subjected the people to all the kingdoms around them, causing them to be a source of shame and desolation to the surrounding nations.

Baruch implored the Lord to turn his anger away from the few remaining Israelites and to deliver them for the Lord's own sake. He asked for the Lord to grant them favor in the eyes of their captors and to let all the earth know that the Lord is their God. Baruch asked the Lord to look down from his holy habitation, hear their prayer and supplication, and incline his ear to their cries. He recognized that the dead in Hades will not be able to ascribe glory or justice to the Lord, but those in distress, those who are hungry and weak, will be able to do so. Baruch acknowledged that their fathers and kings were a stiff-necked people and that it was not because of any righteous deeds that they were seeking mercy from the Lord. He hoped that the people would eventually return to themselves in exile and know that the Lord is their God, giving them a heart that obeys and ears that hear.

Baruch encouraged Jerusalem to take off her garment of grief and affliction and put on the splendour of God's glory forever. He called for Jerusalem to put on the robe of God's righteousness and the diadem of everlasting glory, as God will display her majesty throughout the universe. God will call her "peace of righteousness and glory of godliness" forever. Baruch envisioned Jerusalem ascending to the heights and seeing her children gathered from the east and the west, rejoicing that God has remembered them at the word of the Holy One. God will lead Israel with joy, in the light of his glory, with the mercy and righteousness that come from him. He ordered that every high mountain and everlasting hills be made low and the valleys filled up, so that Israel may walk safely in the glory of God. The woods and fragrant trees will shade Israel at God's command.

In conclusion, Baruch's book was a call for the people of Israel and Judah to remember the Lord their God, turn away from their wicked deeds, and seek mercy and deliverance from the Lord. He encouraged them to put on the splendor of God's glory and walk in the light of his righteousness, for God would lead them with joy and bring them back to Jerusalem in glory.

First and Second Maccabees

The First and Second Maccabees are books included in the Apocrypha, a collection of Jewish texts written between the end of the Old Testament and the beginning of the New Testament. The First Maccabees recounts the history of the Jewish revolt against the Seleucid Empire in the 2nd century BCE and the establishment of the Hasmonean dynasty. The Second Maccabees provides a more detailed account of the same events, as well as additional information on the oppression of the Jews by the Seleucid king, Antiochus IV.

In both books, the focus is on the heroism and faith of the Maccabean brothers, Judas, Simon, Jonathan, and John, who led the rebellion against Antiochus IV and his attempts to force the Jews to abandon their religious practices. The First Maccabees highlights the military victories of the Maccabees, including the recapture of the Temple in Jerusalem and the rededication of the altar, a celebration which became known as Hanukkah. The Second Maccabees, on the other hand, focuses on the miraculous events surrounding the Temple's rededication and the courage of those who suffered and died for their faith.

Both First and Second Maccabees are important historical sources for the period of Jewish history they cover, and they also contain themes that are significant for later Jewish and Christian communities. For example, the books emphasize the importance of maintaining religious practices in the face of persecution and the enduring power of God's promises to his people. The books also illustrate the bravery and determination of those who stood up for their faith, and the importance of passing down their stories from generation to generation.

First and Second Maccabees are valuable additions to the Apocrypha, providing insight into the history and religious beliefs of the Jewish people during a time of great upheaval and oppression.

After vanquishing Darius, King of Persians and Medes, Alexander, the son of Philip from Kittim, claimed the throne and became the new ruler. He had already been crowned as the King of Greece. Alexander engaged in numerous battles, took control of fortresses, and eliminated the rulers of the earth. He embarked on journeys to the far-flung regions of the world, pillaging multiple nations. He basked in glory as the earth submitted to him and his heart swelled with pride. He amassed a formidable army and reigned over a multitude of countries, nations, and rulers, who all became his subjects. However, he soon fell ill and thought his death was near. He called for his most esteemed officers, who had grown up with him, and divided his kingdom among them while he still lived. After twelve years of reign, Alexander passed away. His officers then took over as rulers, each in their own designated regions.

Antiochus returned after conquering Egypt in the 143rd year and went to war against Israel. He marched a huge force to Jerusalem and entered the sanctuary with arrogance, taking the golden altar, the lampstand, and all the utensils. He also removed the table for the bread of Presence, drink offering cups, bowls, censers, curtains, crowns, and gold decorations from the temple entrance. He snatched the silver, gold, and valuable items, along with any secret treasures he discovered. He took everything and went back to his homeland. He committed murder and spoke in a haughty manner. Every community in Israel was inconsolable and the rulers and elders groaned, the young men and maidens fainted, and the women's beauty faded. Every bridegroom bemoaned and brides in the bridal chamber mourned. The land shook as its inhabitants trembled, and the entire house of Jacob was shrouded in shame. Two years later, the king sent a chief collector of tribute to the cities of Judah, who came to Jerusalem with a large army and stationed there a lawless and sinful people. They strengthened their position, stored weapons, and food, and took the spoils of Jerusalem and stored them there. They became a great trap. They became an adversary of the sanctuary, a constant evil for Israel.

They shed innocent blood on every side of the sanctuary and even defiled it. The residents of Jerusalem fled and the city became a dwelling for strangers, alien to her descendants and forsaken by her children. The king then commanded his kingdom to unite as one people and abandon their traditions. His command was accepted by all the Gentiles, and many Israelites adopted his religion, offering sacrifices to idols, profaning the Sabbath, and committing unclean and profane acts, forgetting the law and changing the ordinances. He warned that anyone who did not obey the king's command would face death. He addressed his kingdom with these words and appointed inspectors over the entire population and ordered the cities of Judah to offer sacrifices one by one. They offered sacrifices on the altar of burnt offering on the 25th day of the month. According to the king's decree, those who circumcised their children, along with their families and those who performed the circumcision, were put to death, and infants were hung from their mothers' necks. However, many Israelites remained steadfast in their resolve not to eat unclean food, choosing death over defilement and holy covenant violation, and thus died. God's wrath fell heavily on Israel. Alexander Epiphanes, Antiochus' son, arrived and took control of Ptolemais in the 166th year, where he was welcomed and immediately started ruling.

Second Maccabees

The Jewish brothers and sisters in Jerusalem and Judea send greetings and well wishes for peace to their Egyptian Jewish brothers and sisters. They pray that God will bless and remember his covenant with Abraham, Isaac, and Jacob, give them all a heart to worship him and a willing spirit to follow his will, open their hearts to his law and commandments, and bring peace to their lives. The Jewish community acknowledges the debt of gratitude they owe to God for saving them from certain death by siding with them against the king, who expelled those who opposed the holy city.

The Jewish people recount a story of a deception employed by the priests of Nanea that led to the defeat of an irresistible force led by the leader of Persia. The descendants of the priests were later commissioned by the king of Persia to retrieve the fire in the temple of Nanea. Instead, they found a thick liquid which was used to start a fire during a sacrifice.

The Jews recall the injustice of the murder of Onias, a man who was a benefactor and protector of his fellow countrymen and a zealot for the laws. The murder was caused by the rivalry between Simon, who slandered Onias, and Onias. The king of the time was grieved at the murder and punished the murderer, Andronicus.

The Jews also recount the story of Antiochus, who attempted to rob the temples in Persepolis and was defeated by the people. He learned of the defeat of Nicanor and Timothy's forces and turned on the Jews in anger. Antiochus was boastful and was eventually seized with a pain in his bowels as a result of his arrogance. Three years later, Judas and his men received news of the arrival of Demetrius, the son of Seleucus, who had taken possession of the country. The story ends with the mention of a certain Alcimus.

Additions to the Book of Esther

The book of Esther, also known as the Book of Esther or the Megillat Esther, is one of the books of the Apocrypha, a collection of Jewish texts that were not included in the canon of the Hebrew Bible. The book of Esther is a historical account of the events leading up to the deliverance of the Jewish people in the Persian Empire from a planned extermination. The story takes place in the reign of King Xerxes (Ahasuerus) in the fifth century BCE, and it focuses on a beautiful young Jewish woman named Esther, who becomes the queen of Persia.

The book of Esther begins with a six-month feast held by King Xerxes in Susa, the capital of the Persian Empire. During the feast, the king orders his queen, Vashti, to appear before him, but she refuses. As a result, the king removes her from her position and searches for a new queen. Esther, who was adopted by her cousin Mordecai, is chosen to be the new queen. Meanwhile, a court official named Haman becomes enraged when Mordecai refuses to bow to him and convinces the king to issue a decree ordering the extermination of all Jews in the Persian Empire.

Mordecai learns of the decree and urges Esther to reveal her Jewish identity to the king and plead for the salvation of her people. Esther courageously approaches the king, revealing that she is a Jew, and pleads for the salvation of her people. The king, moved by her bravery, issues a new decree allowing the Jews to defend themselves and their families against their enemies. On the 13th of Adar, the Jews successfully defend themselves and their families, and Haman and his ten sons are executed.

The book of Esther is significant in Jewish tradition as it highlights the role of divine intervention in the events of history and the bravery of the Jewish people in the face of danger. The story is celebrated during the Jewish holiday of Purim, which commemorates the deliverance of the Jews from their enemies. The book of Esther also emphasizes the importance of maintaining Jewish identity and solidarity, even in a foreign land.

Overall, the book of Esther is a powerful reminder of the triumph of the Jewish people over adversity and the resilience of the human spirit in the face of danger:

Mordecai, of the Benjamin tribe, son of Jair, grandson of Shimei, and great-grandson of Kish, had a dream that revealed what God had planned. In his dream, Mordecai saw two mighty dragons approach, bellowing ferociously, as nations prepared for war against the righteous nation. The earth was shrouded in darkness, turmoil, and distress, and the mighty were devoured while the humble were lifted up.

Mordecai stumbled upon a dangerous plot against King Artaxerxes, hatched by two eunuchs, and quickly informed the king. After their confession and execution, the king appointed Mordecai to serve in his court and recorded the events. But despite his newfound position, Haman, son of Hammedatha of Bougaea, who was held in high esteem by the king, plotted to harm Mordecai.

King Artaxerxes sent letters to the rulers of the hundred and twenty-seven provinces from India to Ethiopia, expressing his desire for peace and stability in his kingdom. He feared that a people with differing laws and customs could harm his kingdom and disrupt its tranquility. But Mordecai prayed to the Lord and called to mind his great works, affirming that if it was God's will, no one could stand in his way.

The queen, in her radiant beauty and apparent happiness, was in fact frozen with fear. The king comforted her, assuring her that she would not come to harm as the law applied only to people. In a letter to the rulers of the provinces, King Artaxerxes declared his intention to make his kingdom peaceful and secure for all and condemned the wicked actions of those in power who sought to harm his subjects and conspired against their own benefactors.

However, Haman sought the destruction of Mordecai and Esther, the queen, along with their entire nation, using deceit and cunning. But Mordecai saw these events as coming from God and spoke of the great signs and wonders that God had performed, declaring that Israel would celebrate these days of deliverance and vindication in the month of Adar, on the fourteenth and fifteenth of the month, with joy and gladness before God.

Additions to the Book of Daniel (Susanna, the Prayer of Azariah, and Bel and the Dragon)

The Book of Daniel is a historical and apocalyptic work that centers around the Jewish prophet and advisor to Babylonian King Nebuchadnezzar, Daniel. The book is comprised of two distinct parts: historical stories and visions of the future. Specifically, the Book is revered for its depiction of the faithful and its visions of the future, which were interpreted by early Christians as prophesying the arrival of the Messiah and the establishment of God's kingdom on earth. The book continues to be a source of inspiration and encouragement for those who seek to remain steadfast in their faith, even in the face of persecution and adversity.

The first half of the book contains six historical tales that relate to the lives of Daniel and his friends Hananiah, Mishael, and Azariah. These stories depict the bravery and faith of the young men as they refuse to abandon their religious practices despite being forced into the service of a pagan king. They remain steadfast in their beliefs and are rewarded with divine protection and success.

The second half of the book is comprised of visions and prophecies of the future. These visions depict the rise and fall of various empires and the ultimate triumph of God's kingdom. They include the famous dream of the statue with its feet of iron and clay and the vision of the beasts arising from the sea. The book ends with the story of the resurrection of the dead and the judgment of humanity, with the righteous receiving eternal life and the wicked receiving eternal punishment.

The story as presented in Bel and the Dragon

King Astyages passed away and Cyrus the Persian inherited the kingdom, with Daniel as one of the king's companions and highly regarded friends. The Babylonians worshiped an idol named Bel, lavishing it with daily offerings of twelve bushels of fine flour, forty sheep, and fifty gallons of wine. The king was a devout follower, visiting Bel daily for worship. But Daniel worshiped the true living God, and when the king questioned him about not worshiping Bel, he explained his belief in the almighty creator of heaven and earth.

The king challenged Daniel, threatening to execute him if the priests could not prove Bel was a living deity consuming the offerings. Daniel agreed, and when they entered Bel's temple, the king was shocked to find the footprints of the priests who had been secretly eating the offerings. The king had the priests and their families killed and gave Bel over to Daniel to be destroyed.

The Babylonians also worshiped a great dragon, and the king instructed Daniel to worship it. But Daniel declined and, with the king's permission, killed the dragon without using a weapon by feeding it cakes made of pitch, fat, and hair, causing it to explode. The Babylonians turned on the king, accusing him of becoming a Jew and destroying their sacred beliefs. Under pressure, the king was forced to hand Daniel over to be thrown into the lions' den for six days without food for the lions.

But the Lord had other plans, sending the prophet Habakkuk to bring food to Daniel in the den. Although Habakkuk was unfamiliar with Babylon and the lions' den, he obeyed the Lord's commands and delivered the food, saving Daniel from harm.